THE
POWER
OF POETRY

EQUALITY THE FUTURE HOPE POWER IDENTITY POLLUTION BULLYING DISCRIMINATION WAR POVERTY DISASTER DESTRUCTION

Voices Of Youth

Edited By Debbie Killingworth

First published in Great Britain in 2023 by:

Young Writers
Remus House
Coltsfoot Drive
Peterborough
PE2 9BF
Telephone: 01733 890066
Website: www.youngwriters.co.uk

Printed and bound in the UK by BookPrintingUK
Website: www.bookprintinguk.com
YB0528AZ

FOREWORD

Since 1991, here at Young Writers we have celebrated the awesome power of creative writing, especially in young adults where it can serve as a vital method of expressing their emotions and views about the world around them. In every poem we see the effort and thought that each student published in this book has put into their work and by creating this anthology we hope to encourage them further with the ultimate goal of sparking a life-long love of writing.

Our latest competition for secondary school students, **The Power of Poetry,** challenged young writers to consider what was important to them and how to express that using the power of words. We wanted to give them a voice, the chance to express themselves freely and honestly, something which is so important for these young adults to feel confident and listened to. They could give an opinion, highlight an issue, consider a dilemma, impart advice or simply write about something they love. There were no restrictions on style or subject so you will find an anthology brimming with a variety of poetic styles and topics. We hope you find it as absorbing as we have.

We encourage young writers to express themselves and address subjects that matter to them, which sometimes means writing about sensitive or contentious topics. If you have been affected by any issues raised in this book, details on where to find help can be found at
www.youngwriters.co.uk/info/other/contact-lines

CONTENTS

Dylan Lees (12)	63
Sophia Bath (11)	64
Amelie Patani (13)	65
Ameya Hudson (13)	66
Ashwin Sudan (12)	67
Issa Keval (13)	68
Lola Hollingworth (13)	69
Lewis Clark	70
Daniel Boyle (13)	71
Summer Smith	72
Elsie Cattell	73
Harvey Exton-Johnson (13)	74
Ella Duffy (12)	75
Zachary Taylor (13)	76
Izzy Chick (12)	77
James Yates (12)	78
Emily Morgan (11)	79

Islamia Girls' School, London

Asiya Saqib (15)	80
Siddiqah Maria Khan (15)	82
Maryam M Abdulrahman (16)	84
Amina Omer-Hashi (15)	85
Zahira Khan (15)	86

Ludlow CE School, Ludlow

Lottie Carpenter (15)	87
Esme Hodnett (13)	88

North West Surrey Short Stay School - Kingsway Centre, Woking

Talha Mojid (12)	89

Outwood Academy City, Sheffield

Etana-Rae Blake (12)	90
Brandon Young (11)	92
Desiree Costa (11)	93
Heidi McKay (11)	94
Olivia Yates-Sykes (11)	95

Michaela Hopwood (11)	96
Violet Berry (11)	98
Lily Hussain (12)	99
Khloe Shirley (11)	100
Finlay Wood (14)	101
Dylan Whitehead (13)	102
Summer Shaw (12)	103
Krystal Garner (11)	104
Loui Roberts (13)	105
Leah Grayson (13)	106
Layton Lowe (11)	107
Imogen Mugombe (13)	108
Grace Haythorne (11)	109
Luke Whyers (11)	110
Zac Sylvester (13)	111
Tallulah Marples (11)	112
Kaiden Newall (12)	113
Maleek Kadir (11)	114
Alfie King (13)	115
Logan Parker (11)	116
Jade Ledgerwood (13)	117
Jacob Ellis (13)	118
Lucas Thompson (12)	119
Chloe Tonks (13)	120

Outwood Academy Normanby, Middlesbrough

Lilly-May Pell (14)	121
Grace Brown (12)	122
Honey Pattison (12)	125
LilyMay Larsen (11)	126
Sophia Siraj (11)	128
Olivia Perry (11)	129
Elexie Lynes (12)	130
Ollie McGarry (12)	131
Bethany Quinn (12)	132
Liam Daniels (12)	133
Tanisha Sellars (11)	134
Faith McGarry (13)	135
Layla-Rose Spence (12)	136
Millie Brown (12)	137
Nancy Brookes (11)	138
Emily Mcroy (14)	139

Lacee Thompson (11)	140
Riley Henderson (11)	141
Willow Rose Thompson (11)	142
Charlie Hanley (11)	143

Serlby Park Academy, Bircotes

| Eve Cox (11) | 144 |
| Hayden Squire (11) | 146 |

St George's College Weybridge, Addlestone

Allegra Cesar (12)	147
Mila Elahi (11)	148
Maya Pozina (12)	150
Scout Westen (12)	152
Alice Dines (11)	154
Frank Challouma (11)	156
Ted Langrish (11)	157
Jessica Rolton (11)	158
Finlay Bolah (12)	159
Alexia Mattina (12)	160
Emma Muraszko (11)	161
Thomas Wolf (12)	162
Amy Cotterell (12)	163
Siena Lenman (11)	164
Ben Puddephatt (12)	165
Max Brindley (11)	166
Juliana Lima (11)	167
Sophia Jory (12)	168
Sammy Hooper (11)	169
Ben Fellows (11)	170
Tobiah Eldridge (12)	171
Filip Matejka (11)	172
Beth Harrison (12)	173
Aidan Geraghty (12)	174
Bonnie Young (13)	175
Johanna Martius-Jones (11)	176
Ishwer Najjhur (11)	177
Enid Howes Barley (11)	178
James Pittard (11)	179
Emily Wainwright (11)	180
Emma Lee (12)	181

Isobel Bokenham (12)	182
Florence Langlands (11)	183
Sebastian Edwards (11)	184
Gabriella Hern (12)	185
Oscar Ryan (12)	186
Jacques Marais (11)	187
Emilia Bownds (11)	188
Katie-Mae Hogg (11)	189
Jessica Hooper (12)	190
Jasper Gill (12)	191
Connor Duckworth (12)	192
Benjamin Kay (12)	193
Louis Bortnik (11)	194
Sofia Stotter-Brooks (12)	195
Oscar Sibley (11)	196
George Davis (11)	197
Tessa Gerber (11)	198
Mark Morcos (11)	199
Rory Hotchkiss (13)	200

St Patrick's RC High School & Arts College, Eccles

Aryanna Madzura (11)	201
Munachi Unagha (14)	202
Alex Sobczyk (11)	204
Megan Cochrane (11)	206
Katie Ratcliffe (13)	207
Kyra Mason (12)	208
Lourdez Francis (12)	209
Adrian Rojek (13)	210
Magdalena Goluchowska (14)	211

The McAuley Catholic High School, Doncaster

Connie Rushton (15)	212
Maja Lada (15)	214
Lottie White (14)	215
Georgie Pratt (16)	216
Frankie Bergmanas (13)	218

THE
POEMS

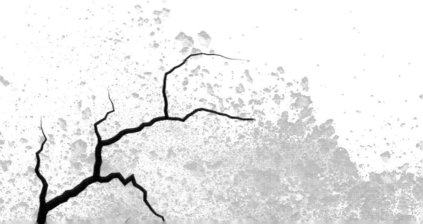

The Epic Game

Online we fly to the line we love
We shoot to the sky to destroy
And shoot down like a volcano rocket
Filled up with power.

My friends, shooting to win
In the epic game for the legendaries
As I ride to the death I lead my team to the win
As we dance, I stand
As I draw my sword and say, "Well done."

Jay (13)

Litter

How would you feel if the streets you were stepping on were
dirty and filled with litter?
Let's stop litter,
Let's make Earth glitter,
If you listen to me, you will glisten the world.

This won't only benefit us,
But it will also make seas and rivers clear,
Which will be appealing to hear,
Unpolluted, ultramarine blue,
Makes the environment calmer,
It makes the environment healthier.

Recycling will also retain natural materials
And make streets better,
Allow animals to live longer and safer,
Make oceans cleaner,
and grass greener.

This is good for the environment
And it's also very hygienic,
It will make streets flickering and polished,
It will make Earth gleam and lustrous.

Shaarav Dalal
Abbeyfield School, Northampton

Despondent Ocean

Swallowed by an ocean, far below
Waves drown out my broken song,
A struggle for help, and a wish for freedom
Crushed by the pressure of solitude.

The warmth of the sun on the beach with my friends,
The smiles we shared, the troubles we bared,
The jubilant time of our youth,
The time when I felt free.

Bit by bit, the clock's hands turned,
Friendships gone blank, suffocated by time,
Tripping and stumbling, alone and worried,
Sinking deeper and deeper into the murky seas.

The sun's rays blackened, its warmth reduced to nil,
My forlorn self encroached by the water,
I cry invisible tears, I bellow a false laugh,
All drowned out by my despondent ocean.

Alpher Gwenzi (15)
Abbeyfield School, Northampton

Bullies And The Bullied

I cry every day
Because of the one called bullies
I always wonder, what do they go through?
There is a reason
There is always a reason
That they are cruel
I despise them
They are like a pack of vicious wolves
But what is it that makes them like this?
There is a secret deep inside that tells a story
A dark story of their life
Sometimes I pity them, it is hard to be them
I always thought they must have gone through worse
Worse than ever imagined
If only that was just it
But it is not
A portion of them do it just for the pleasure
Quite sad for the bullied, right?
Is it not?

Temitayo Olarewaju (11)
Bishop Perowne CE College, Worcester

Freedom

Freedom is like a dog without a leash,
Always running free,
Never knowing what will happen next.

Freedom is a never-ending hope,
Once in sight it can never be taken away.

Freedom is the light
That leads you to your safe place.

Freedom is whatever you want it to be,
Just believe and you will find your way
And once you find it never let it go.

Keira Cale (14)
Bishop Perowne CE College, Worcester

Lewa (Beauty)

I just want to walk
Walk slow
Not low, with inspiration for my next show
Up on a hill
Pen and book in hand
Ah yes, the cold breeze that blows with the sand
In all directions hitting my face and cooling it down
Grass green as my lawn
With all my might I write until the night
Growing is knowing that as the sun leaves the green dims.

Tomi Olarewaju (15)
Bishop Perowne CE College, Worcester

My First New Day

Walking into the classroom, faces everywhere
Me faffing, trying to fix my hair
All the faces new and bright
All staring at me, giving me a fright
The teacher stands up and introduces me
Saying to the class I'm as sweet as a pea
Seven years later, I still remember this day
And all I was thinking was *I want to run away.*

She told me to sit down
Next to the tall kid, who had a horrible frown
As soon as I sat in my seat
The chair was towering, I lost my feet
We were told to draw a mouse
I also drew a big brown house
Seven years later I still remember this day
And all I was thinking was, *this is nice, can I stay?*

Now it was break time
I need to make some friends of mine
I wandered over to a bench to see
A large group following me
They just wanted to play
And I said, "Yes you may"
Seven years later I remember this day
And all I was thinking was *hip hip hooray!*

Abby Hooper (14)
Brookvale Groby Learning Campus, Groby

Sad Little Bee

As I lie in the dizzying sun
That warms the tips of my hair
The golden sunset spilling into my room
I lie and reflect on my day...
The way it went
The way I wanted it to go
I wanted to laugh today
And have fun with my friends at school
I just want to be as happy as a bee
Without a care in the world
But that's not reality, is it?
Because today, I felt ashamed
Ashamed to be me, an outcast
For I was called names
On my own
All on my own, alone
Causing the anxiety to slither up to my neck
Constricting it
And I try to pull it off
With all my might
I try
Because I can't breathe
Or see
But I can't cry
I can't be seen as weak

My world comes crashing down
And I wake up here in my bed
Feeling low
So low
But when I open my computer
To write my own world
That I can control
And listen to music
The dark clouds that once oppressed me
Begin to fade
And I'm me again
And I cry
I feel better
I feel human
I feel me.

Imogen Leatherland (14)
Brookvale Groby Learning Campus, Groby

Our Home

The world is our home,
The vibrant olive trees
That change colour each season,
Bringing us joy when we see them,
Dancing in the wind.
The scintillating blue sky,
That watches down on all of us.
The shimmering ocean,
Reflecting the glow of the sun,
Sparkling and clear.
We can breathe, live and feel,
But one by one we are destroying
The only things that keep us alive.

The glistening ocean,
Now grey and bleak,
Plastic filling it like a wasteland.
The plastic that once sealed our food.
The ocean that witnessed the growth
Has witnessed the now killing of our home.

The trees that sway,
In the breeze of the wind.
Gone. Dead. Gone. Murdered.
The sky that holds our sun,
Is being polluted,

By the cars we drive,
That take us to the places we love.

One step, one breath,
Our actions will follow us.
And soon our home will fall,
Taking us deeper into the disaster,
We caused in the first place.

Amy Lennox (13)
Brookvale Groby Learning Campus, Groby

I Hate Poems

Poetry I don't like.
It's quite simple, more than riding a bike.
I hate that saying, I'm sure you know it...
'I'm a poet and I didn't know it'.
I also hate James,
He gives me eye pains.
Generally English is bad,
It makes me sad.
I hate what, how, why paragraphs,
I want to cry.
I'm not even going to lie.
However, I love having a Sub,
It's a major dub.
I also hate cinnamon swirls.
I'm always first to read, it makes my toes curl.
I'm happy I won't have English for a week,
But when I come back it's gonna peak.
Usually I just stare into space
But when the bell goes it lights up my face.
Ring, ring, ring, ding, ding sing, sing!

Phoebe Paddison (13)
Brookvale Groby Learning Campus, Groby

What I Find Scary

Spiders are scary, aren't they?
The eyes and eight legs might fool you
Even though many of them can't be cruel to you.

Heights are scary, aren't they?
They just make you want to stay down
They make you want to turn around
And you feel like they will hurt you now.

Clowns are scary, aren't they?
They try to make you happy
But your face ends up with a frown
And you feel like they're taking away your personal crown
And you don't feel like they should be allowed.

Bugs are scary, aren't they?
They are called creepy crawlies for a reason
Terrified people feel like they have committed high treason
Even though they want to be left alone.

Charlie Hickinbotham (13)
Brookvale Groby Learning Campus, Groby

Football

Football is the best
Who will win next?
Man City? Man United?

The big debate
Messi or Ronaldo
They both get hate.

The thrill of the crowd
Makes team fans very proud.

A dream to be pro
Keep training and go with the flow
Making lots of money
Earning millions because it's funny.

Mbappé wants Neymar out
That causes Pochettino to shout.

Kane doing a knee slide celebration
Also crying happiness for his nation.

Big signings for clubs
Managers hoping to bring their teams up.

Man City, top of the table they are
More points than Liverpool by far.

Fans dream to get more points
On the fantasy football team.

Louie Wood (13)
Brookvale Groby Learning Campus, Groby

Football Isn't Just A Sport

Football is more than just a sport to me,
It's more than just kicking a ball or watching it on TV,
Although I enjoy the atmosphere's electricity,
Playing the sport makes me feel even more happy,
A lot more than experiencing it on the telly,
For me I love it when I score,
And making passing plays through the air and on the floor,
Tracking back to stop their attack,
Once I'm playing for the club I will never slack,
I would die for that badge even though
There's little chance I will make it pro,
But that doesn't bother me,
Football just makes me happy,
That's why football is more than just a sport to me.

Tate Ramsell (14)
Brookvale Groby Learning Campus, Groby

My Days In Foundation

Nothing lasts forever,
Things change as frequently as the weather,
I remember my days in foundation,
So much fun at the water station.

The many books I would write,
Attempting to reach greater heights,
And though they weren't great
Many rewards were my fate.

Playing outside on the tyres,
Leaving drills for fires,
Having fun with my friends,
A happiness that never ends.

However, when I was seven,
I was pulled out from my little heaven,
For it was time to move,
Many friends I did lose.

And when I left there was a celebration,
To forever remember my days in foundation.

Joshua Bampton (12)
Brookvale Groby Learning Campus, Groby

Love For Football

Football is an amazing sport, isn't it?
It's amazing what people can do.
Dribble with such fast feet,
Make people look incomplete.
The skills that they pull off
Make people want to hide in a loft.
The shots make people rot,
The saves keepers make are amazing!

Three points, it's what matters the most,
For next Saturday when we face our next host.
Top of the table we are,
This journey is still quite far,
Thinking of holding the trophy in my hands,
While there is uproar in the stands.
We love this team,
We hope it's not a dream,
To win the Premier League.

Brendan Knight (13)
Brookvale Groby Learning Campus, Groby

Pampa

Time is important.
Memories are too.
Because when people are gone, they don't come back to
you.
Take my pampa.
Pampa was always kind, if a little bit naughty.
He has always been very important to me.
Like memories from when I was smaller.

Eating crab on the Cornwall coast.
Him coming round for Sunday roast.
Feeding the dogs biscuits on the settee.
Him sneakily giving chocolate to me.
Tickling us until we would scream.
Him buying me raspberry ripple ice cream.

So much time together, but not quite enough.
Spend time with your loved ones and fill it with love.

Georgia Hope (12)
Brookvale Groby Learning Campus, Groby

Pollution

The pollution, all in the sky,
The smell, the feel, it's awful.
Comes from cars and power plants
And we're killing the trees and bees, stop it!
It's here, it's there, it's everywhere.
Producing CO2 just for money for a yacht.
Causing the greenhouse effect and sea rising.
And the water rushing up and people wandering.
So just keep that CO2 neutral!
And we can't produce absolutely 0 of it
Because the world would have to change completely.
We can't flick a switch overnight
But we can over time.

Samuel Halford (12)
Brookvale Groby Learning Campus, Groby

Little Cousins

Little cousins, they're the best, aren't they?
Always screaming or want to play.
Running around tripping over little things,
Or pretending their fake phones ping.
Little cousins, they're the best, aren't they?

They never sit still and rest,
Sometimes our patience they really test.
Always wanting biscuits or treats,
Or listening to music which they call beats.
Little cousins, they're the best, aren't they?

Sometimes they act like teenagers at ten,
But in the end, we really love them.

Sophie Cannaby (13)
Brookvale Groby Learning Campus, Groby

That Car

I always praised that car
But now it's probably very far.
That car, oh that car,
I always loved that car.
The beautiful engine thrusting and driving that power,
That car was amazing, and how you could use that V8 power.
The aerodynamics, slicing through the air like a knife through butter, it was swift,
Any use was fit whether racing a drag or giving a friend a lift.
Whether camping on the side of a mountain,
Or guzzling gas at the petrol fountain.
0-60 in 3, 2, 1... go!
And bam! It's there in one blow.

Aryan Shubh Parekh (13)
Brookvale Groby Learning Campus, Groby

The Patchwork Leaves

I sit at the rusty bus stop,
Waiting to be picked up,
Alone, on my own.

As the crisp autumn breeze blew my golden locks,
The patchwork leaves flew and greeted me
As I gradually stood up.

The others darted around me like dogs seeing their owner
After a rough day at work.

Delighted, intrigued, astounded,
I bowed to the kind souls
As we danced under the illuminating lamp posts.

Although my bus arrived
And they all cascaded to the cobble floor
And yet again I stood alone.

Isabella Barr (11)
Brookvale Groby Learning Campus, Groby

Christmas

Christmas! There are presents and peas,
Isn't it amazing? So much to say!
There are Christmas tops, turkey and trees
And children just wanting to play.

Wonderful! Don't you agree?
Resting by the fire after being drenched in snow.
There are displays everywhere for all to see,
And Santa at night, shouting, "Ho ho ho!"

But most of all, what I love the best
Is the part I'm with my family!
My cousins who won't give it a rest,
And aunties and uncles decorating a tree.

Esmé Mackay (12)
Brookvale Groby Learning Campus, Groby

High School Is Hard

High school is hard,
The kids don't make it easier.
They stare, they laugh,
I try to ignore it.

I just want to be myself,
Without being bothered
But people are cruel, people are mean,
So I doubt it's possible.

If I'm not perfect, I'm dead meat.
One mistake and they shout,
One shout and I cry,
One cry and they laugh,
One laugh and I die.

I can't show any emotion
Or they'll kill me.
High school is hard,
It isn't easy.

Olly De-Rosa (14)
Brookvale Groby Learning Campus, Groby

I Love Space

I love space!
I love how rockets go fast like a race!
And when they went to the moon
Neil Armstrong left a trace...
The footprint.
Don't look at the sun
Because your eyes will hurt and you have to squint.
I wonder what moondust tastes like?
Maybe it tastes like mint!
Space is freezing but that's why I like it,
I think it's so amazing.
Because sound doesn't travel through space.
I wonder if you can even hear some whistling.
I love space and planets.

Jacob Doyle (13)
Brookvale Groby Learning Campus, Groby

Christmas

Snow falls every December,
I need gloves, scarves and coats to remember.
Putting up the tree makes me jolly,
Decorating the house full of holly.

Wrapping tinsel around my tree,
Bauble after bauble makes the room glee.
Unwrapping presents and opening gifts,
People seeing family, getting a lift.

Watching Home Alone, getting cosy and snug,
Drinking hot chocolate out of my favourite mug.
Elves helping Santa Claus,
Waiting for the children to applaud.

Ella Mistry
Brookvale Groby Learning Campus, Groby

Football

Football is great,
No matter what place.
If you're a boy or a girl,
The best sport in the world.

The roar of a crowd,
What a spectacular sound.
The echoing of chants,
Might make you dance.

The celebration of a goal,
Or a save with heart and soul.
A signature celebration,
After a goal for your home nation.

Watching your favourite club,
Hoping they play the star sub.
If they play the game,
The world knows your name.

Darcey Sergent (13)
Brookvale Groby Learning Campus, Groby

I Love Football

I love football,
Gonna be pro,
Making loads of dough.
The thrill of the crowd,
Chanting so loud,
Making people proud,
Gotta train hard,
Not hitting the bar,
Buying my favourite car,
I love football.

Doing my celebration,
For my nation,
Black and white's my team,
That would be my dream,
Playing for Derby County,
Not eating Bountys,
Top of the league we are,
Even though our journey's far,
I love football.

Sid Crooks
Brookvale Groby Learning Campus, Groby

I Am Pollution

I am the world's worst nightmare,
Try and stop me if you dare.
Eat less meat and recycle more paper
But you are too late to stop the planet hater.
I have melted the ice caps
And in the ozone layer there are gaps.
I have followed mankind's instruction
Which has led to the planet's destruction.
If you want to help prevent me
Maybe consider planting a tree.
It doesn't have to end this way,
You can make small changes and save the day.

Noah Phipps (11)
Brookvale Groby Learning Campus, Groby

It's The Little Things In Life

It's the little things in life,
They mean the most to me.
When you feel down,
Smile, don't frown,
And remember all those happy things.
Shopping with your friends,
Playing pretend.
Maybe eating out with your family,
Maybe buying slushies or playing hide-and-seek.
Life isn't just a rainy day,
Sometimes bad thoughts can get in the way.
But, just think of all the little things that make you happy
And it might just make your day!

Alyssia Dale (12)
Brookvale Groby Learning Campus, Groby

The Ocean

You don't know what's lurking in the depths of the ocean.
It's deep and dark with weird creatures swimming in the
murky water.
There are skinny sharks and fat fish with big black eyes.
Something could come from beneath and bite you with its
teeth.
You could be paddling peacefully when something appears
in front of you and makes you jump and your heart thump.
The ocean is deep and scary, so beware when you swim, as
the water will make your legs grow hairy!

Isabelle White

Brookvale Groby Learning Campus, Groby

Never Give Up

Rule number one, never give up,
Football affects my everyday life.
I wasn't interested, until two years ago,
Now I love it, that I know.
Pulling my socks up, tying my hair back,
Getting ready for a big match.
Atmosphere was high,
Intensity at its finest.
Dribbling the ball at my feet, running down the wing,
The crowd screaming, "Keep going!"
Shooting, scoring, smiling on my debut,
My dad's dreams had just come true.

Ellie Bray (13)
Brookvale Groby Learning Campus, Groby

The War Against The Environment

Will this war ever stop?
There is a shortage of food and of crops.

The trees try not to shrivel up and die,
In-between them, many soldiers lie.

If we look on the bright side though,
I am not dead yet,
I've not been caught by the Nazi net.

Smoke and ash spread around the field,
As plants and animals lay down and yield.

So don't let the globe fight and squabble,
We're leading into a world of trouble.

Tom Dodd (11)
Brookvale Groby Learning Campus, Groby

Winter

Snow trickled down from above,
Gradual and slow, white as a dove,
Cold winter ice flowing into view,
All hearts open, calm and true,
The brightness of summer splintering away,
A new season of weather brought in today,
Shivers of the cold enter the home,
Along comes the winter, a new cheery tone,
Gloves, shoes and warm hats,
Rubbing shoes off on new winter mats,
A work day's now done,
Time to drink hot chocolate by the ton.

Holly Bartlett (12)
Brookvale Groby Learning Campus, Groby

My Dog

My dog is my world,
I love how happy she is all the time.
Her eyes are shiny like a pearl
But she does love to climb!
Sometimes she's a nightmare,
She's very greedy and steals my food.
She always barks and pulls my hair,
But she puts me out of my mood.
I'm so happy when I see her,
Especially after a long day,
I like to stroke her soft, fluffy fur.
If I tell her to lay she does it right away.
This is my dog.

Millie Gibson (12)
Brookvale Groby Learning Campus, Groby

Ten Things In A Musician's Pocket

A chord in a hey, whether it's major or minor
A chromatic scale to make the music finer
A treble of clefs: alto, neutral and bass
A gentle glissando, to give it some grace
A selection of dynamics to fortify the sound
A nimble arpeggio, to thoroughly astound
A mystical trill to satisfy the ear
A staccato or legato for everyone to hear
A quindicesimo alta to challenge the hand
A quartet of quavers to be played on the grand.

Will Lennox (15)
Brookvale Groby Learning Campus, Groby

What Have We Done? What Could We Do?

All of the food that we waste ends up in space.

Have you ever thought about all of the animals that have lost their homes due to deforestation?

Or about the poor birds that have died because they ate plastic?

We could stop the animals dying.

We could all try to recycle more.

Make birdhouses for those poor birds that don't have a home

And only eat the food that we need.

So all of the food that we waste doesn't end up in space.

Evangeline Sarkis (11)

Brookvale Groby Learning Campus, Groby

D&D Isn't Just For Nerds

People say, "Only nerds like D&D."
You can fight, explore and flee.
Whatever you imagine, you can bring to life,
Even raid a village or fly a kite.
There are lots of types of quests,
But I like DMing as it feels the best.
When you think of D&D you wouldn't expect,
Bullies give it their respect.
You think of nerds playing it,
But try it and you'll see,
That it is for everyone including me.

Finlay Clarke (12)

Brookvale Groby Learning Campus, Groby

My Family

I love my family so very much,
I really don't know what I would do without them.
They've been by my side all the way,
Every second and minute of each day.
I am always thankful to my family for supporting me,
Even when they're not around to see.
I wish I could watch back all the memories,
That my family has shared with me.
So what this poem is all about,
Is that I love my family without a doubt.

Jayden Sleath (12)
Brookvale Groby Learning Campus, Groby

The Polar Bear And The Pollution

The polar bear sits on the rotting ice,
Starving, as the fish rapidly go extinct.
This is the effect of pollution,
The water had become an amalgamation of toxins and plastic,
Then the ice cracked as the polar bear was standing on it.
The polar bear fell into the toxins and never came back up.
Only a pile of deformed, melted bones floated to the surface,
And in a couple of seconds an entire species went extinct.

Jack Pattison (11)
Brookvale Groby Learning Campus, Groby

There's No Place Like Rome

I'd never been to a place like Rome,
It was all new but somehow felt like home.

The Colosseum, Trevi Fountain or just beautiful streets
And the delicious food, so much to eat!

I would go back again any time of the year,
Because of the weather and what you can hear.

But mostly because it's the place I love to see,
And the places you love are where you should be.

Isabel Ackland (12)
Brookvale Groby Learning Campus, Groby

Cat Calamity

I have two cats and they are very different,
Both of them have beautiful moss-green eyes,
One is furry and one is fat,
But both love fuss more than I love pies.
One is black and white and the other is pure black,
One is super friendly and the other hates the spotlight.
I love them both and I thought they loved each other too
But I learned my lesson when I first saw them fight.

Charlie Darker (12)

Brookvale Groby Learning Campus, Groby

Spiders

Spiders, spiders,
Eight legs, more,
A thousand eyes
Staring at me.

Hairy legs,
Crawling all over me.
What the little girl saw
Made her bawl.

Cobwebs all over,
Stringy white webs
Thick and thin,
Sticking to everythin'.

The home where spiders lay,
All day, every day,
In the corner, hiding,
Ready to be frightening.

Demi Toon (13)
Brookvale Groby Learning Campus, Groby

Our Earth Is Dying

I am everything that you know
But if you do not treat me carefully I may go.

I am the animals that are screaming and belting
And the ice caps that are shrinking and melting.

So don't ignore that I am here
And help the Earth by telling a peer.

You do not want this to pass through generations
So help your grandchild with a world full of imaginations.

Samuel Bywater (11)
Brookvale Groby Learning Campus, Groby

Litter Trap

I was swimming in the sea
And then some litter caught me.
It pulled me down, way down
Where the water turned brown
And there I was in a tangle
With a thing called a bangle.
This is all because of you,
Now, what will you do?
I tried to spin and to hurtle,
Please save this little sea turtle!
It is all your responsibility.
Will you please come to help me?

Isabelle Clarke (12)
Brookvale Groby Learning Campus, Groby

My Gran

My gran's the best
Helps me to be my best
With a smile on her face
She helps to save my day.

With advice under her belt
She uses it to help me out
I love her without a doubt
And I know she loves me to the moon and back.

We are apart for now
But I'll be back
I love you a lot
We are tied with an invisible knot.

Jake Frain (12)
Brookvale Groby Learning Campus, Groby

The Tree's Voice

City of whispers,
Sympathy of sighs,
Intricate embroidery,
Green treetops high.

The trees talk to me,
Looking deep into my eyes,
Telling me of the mean mankind,
Chop, chop, chop, the trees say they go,
And the truth becomes clear,
I'd knock onto accomplishment's door
And the trees would live no longer in fear.

Maximus Palmer (11)
Brookvale Groby Learning Campus, Groby

The Butterfly

Unaware of the changes in the world
Like climate change and deforestation.

Fluttering around without a care
And peacefully watching the leaves dance in the wind.

Oh how I wish to be a butterfly
And to live so wild and free.

As life as a butterfly would be so great
I can just forget about life and be... me!

Eliza Simmonds (11)
Brookvale Groby Learning Campus, Groby

My Dog

My dog,
She runs around mad and crazy
Or sometimes she's really lazy.

My dog,
Lying around on her back,
She gives her friends pawsome slaps!

My dog,
Stealing things all the time,
Sometimes they are hard to find.

My dog,
Sometimes she's a real pest
But, really she is the best!

Gracie Morris (12)
Brookvale Groby Learning Campus, Groby

The Beautiful Sport

I love the beautiful sport, football.
It calms and relaxes me.
It never fails to help me,
You will never fail to see
How much effort I put in to make this work.
The ball is like a guide in my life.
The teams are amazing, incredible and unstoppable.
The beautiful game and I will never stop the grind.
The beautiful game.

Reiss Frost (12)
Brookvale Groby Learning Campus, Groby

Our Future Is In Our Hands

The world is a harsh place,
Full of blood and war,
Destroying our environment.
In the forest,
Relaxation is disturbed.
Humans.

But mankind isn't always horrid,
People hope,
People believe,
People feel,
"We will win our future."

Action must happen
If we want to stay.

Harry Coupland (11)
Brookvale Groby Learning Campus, Groby

My Twin

My twin is a miracle but sometimes she isn't okay
And her best friend is very mean.
She has a baby cat called Shelby
And she loves her siblings (including me).
Her siblings are like angry snakes.
Crash! Her siblings are messing around again.
Her siblings always fall in the snow,
Their bottoms in the air!

Lucia Bailey (12)
Brookvale Groby Learning Campus, Groby

My Dog

I love my dog!
She is cute and sweet,
I will always hug her
And give her treats.

But behind her sweet eyes,
There lives the devil herself,
She eats sweets and lollipops
With the stick and the wrapper.

I hate my dog!
She is cute and sweet,
I will always hug her
And give her treats.

Natalia Bogus (12)
Brookvale Groby Learning Campus, Groby

School Is Draining

School. It's a jail, isn't it?
It's a prison, hard to stay in.
Every day, school feels more mentally draining,
At some point, my concentration will be fading
But I still have to go every single day.
I would be so happy if there would be a way,
To help children in need,
With their mental health.

Shaan Billan (13)
Brookvale Groby Learning Campus, Groby

Christmas

Christmas is the best time of year
Watching the snowflakes fall near
Hanging decorations on the tree
And going Christmas shopping, my mum and me
The joy of opening presents in the morning
But for some people Christmas might be boring
I love seeing all my family
Because that is what truly makes me happy.

Ava Coupland (12)
Brookvale Groby Learning Campus, Groby

Art

Expression can be whatever,
From acting, writing or singing.
Art has been there since forever,
A way to clear my head.

From painting emotions, landscapes or portraits,
So many different artistic mediums.
Even doodling lakes, eyes or character traits,
Art is my passion and my way of being me.

Daisy Steiner (12)
Brookvale Groby Learning Campus, Groby

Christmas Dream

Santa's sleigh glides
As presents sit by his side
With children's surprise
Lights shine in their eyes
Before they share
The Christmas fayre.

Wrapping paper scrunching
Bellies rumbling
Dad's moaning
And Grandad's struggling
And fiddling with his beard.

Max Ryan (13)
Brookvale Groby Learning Campus, Groby

Lionesses

Lionesses winning
A game that changed the way women and girls were seen
playing football
It made every player equal no matter what
Kelly goes for the shot
Crash! The ball goes in the back of the net
What a shot
The women have done something the men haven't been
able to do.

Emily Fitches (14)

Brookvale Groby Learning Campus, Groby

Protect

The environment needs protecting
Because we are doing the infecting.
Our world as we know it is damaged,
We must stop this carnage.

Solar panels, to project,
Making our world beautiful and bright.
This all stops icebergs melting
Because our environment needs protecting.

Millie Goodwin (11)
Brookvale Groby Learning Campus, Groby

Fight For The Future

Stop the pollution, stop the fires,
Give them an environment.
We can still make a change,
Fight, fight, fight!
Fight for the future,
We will maintain a longer future.
Fight, fight, future fighting!
Toxins, rubbish, metal, food,
Do you think we're doing good?

Rishi Mistry (11)
Brookvale Groby Learning Campus, Groby

New York City

I love New York City
Especially when it's Christmas, it's so pretty.
Walking down streets and leaving footprints in the snow.
I love looking at the Christmas lights glow
But I hate walking down them alone,
Not looking where I'm going, focused on my phone.

Millie Rowe (13)
Brookvale Groby Learning Campus, Groby

Cheese Is 'Grate'

Cheese, it has many flavours.
Red Leicester, Cheddar and maybe Camembert.
It's as necessary as air.
If you find some, eat it quick,
Otherwise I will nick it!
So if you also love cheese, get some now,
Or I will get a cow
And give you some fresh cheese.

Dylan Lees (12)
Brookvale Groby Learning Campus, Groby

My Home Is Melting

My home is melting,
What can I do?
My home is melting,
Because of you.
My home is melting,
Floating out to sea.
My home is melting,
Taking my family.
My home is melting,
But what do you care?
My home is melting,
Help this little bear!

Sophia Bath (11)
Brookvale Groby Learning Campus, Groby

Football Is My Passion

Football is my passion.
From the moment I tie my boots
It reveals all my truths.
Scoring and shooting is my aim
Even if I go through some pain.
Attacking is what I do,
What if we are losing, so?
That's why football is my passion.

Amelie Patani (13)
Brookvale Groby Learning Campus, Groby

I Hate Spiders

I hate spiders
They are ugly and hairy
Creepy crawlies
Very small and scary.

Some are slow
Some are fast
Some are thin
Some are vast.

Spiders, spiders
Such a sin
Why on earth
They always win.

Ameya Hudson (13)
Brookvale Groby Learning Campus, Groby

Racism Matters

Black lives matter,
That's the message,
That's what matters.
Eight minutes, that's all it took
For his life to be taken.
The police surrounded him
And dropped him to the ground.
They started to beat him and pound.

Ashwin Sudan (12)
Brookvale Groby Learning Campus, Groby

I Appreciate Your Friends

My friends are nice, they are funny
And sometimes they are dummies
But my mates are great.
They are happy, sometimes sad
But always glad.
They are happy, sad, glad and mad,
They are great and never late.

Issa Keval (13)
Brookvale Groby Learning Campus, Groby

When I Fell In A Canal

I once fell in a canal
I was eight years old
Riding on my bicycle
Being nosey as usual
Looking at the houses across the canal
I wobbled on my bike
Off the path I went
And into the river I went!

Lola Hollingworth (13)

Brookvale Groby Learning Campus, Groby

Bullying

I hate bullying
It's so upsetting
There is no point
So depressing
It causes kids to self-harm
People take it way too far
So can't we all just be nice
And pay a compliment to a friend?

Lewis Clark
Brookvale Groby Learning Campus, Groby

Football

Football is great.
There are so many things to do
Like running just for fun
Or kicking the ball with my foot
And ending up on my butt.
Sometimes I score
And leave the keeper lying on the floor.

Daniel Boyle (13)
Brookvale Groby Learning Campus, Groby

Rain

Rain, oh how I love the rain,
It's calming, relaxing, peaceful, dreamy,
It drips down the window
Like race cars zooming down the race track.
Rain, rain, rain,
Oh, how I love the rain!

Summer Smith
Brookvale Groby Learning Campus, Groby

Shopping

I love shopping.
Spending money all the time,
Buying new clothes,
Getting new things.

On sunny or rainy days,
With friends or family,
Clothes or make-up,
Inside or out.

Elsie Cattell
Brookvale Groby Learning Campus, Groby

How I Hate Nottingham Forest

Why I hate Forest...
Forest are rivals of Leicester
Forest are awful
Hope they get relegated
Losing 4-0 to bottom of the league
How embarrassing
Your fans must have been snoring.

Harvey Exton-Johnson (13)
Brookvale Groby Learning Campus, Groby

Christmas Spirit

The best time of the year
Decorating a tree
Spreading cheer
Giving gifts
Can't you see?
Seeing family
Lighting candles
The Christmas spirit
Can't you see?

Ella Duffy (12)
Brookvale Groby Learning Campus, Groby

I Like Rugby

Rugby is great.
You can play any time of year.
In the rain, sun, snow, cold
And even on the beach!
You can make new friends
And loads of memories.
Rugby is great.

Zachary Taylor (13)
Brookvale Groby Learning Campus, Groby

Best Friend

Older or younger it doesn't matter.
Your best friend is who you want them to be.
The memories we made,
I will never forget.
And I hope to make some more together soon!

Izzy Chick (12)
Brookvale Groby Learning Campus, Groby

I Love Pets

My pets are helpful
My pets are cool
I have a dog
Two cats too

My dog is furry
My cat is fat
One disappears
And never comes back.

James Yates (12)
Brookvale Groby Learning Campus, Groby

Earth Is Requesting Help

A haiku

Earth needs help right now.
Get off your butt, help needed!
Maybe litter pick?

Emily Morgan (11)
Brookvale Groby Learning Campus, Groby

A Humble Human

A humble human,
Innocent and naive,
Roaming through life; the world is an oyster,
So they say,
But can it speak?

Eyes don't lie and they see it all,
Hear the news as it shouts for help,
Earth shudders, it quakes, it whines, it shakes,
So should we stop and think?

The howls of wind, angered by destruction,
Rain punishing as it razes human trace,
Red-handed we stand proud, with adamant denial;
When will we stop and think?

The cry of tigers, the leopards, gorillas,
The thirst of trophies, of flesh, fur, bone,
Plastic beasts that hunt blameless turtles;
When will we stop and think?

We are eating away the rainforests,
Pouring fuel at the feet of fire,
Becoming Frankensteins, encouraging, pleading chaos;
When will we stop and think?

Chipping away at the world,
A chip, chip, all take,
Fooling ourselves of our generosity;
When will we stop and think?

A humble human,
Innocent and naive,
Roaming through life: the world is an oyster,
So they say,
But it speaks.

Asiya Saqib (15)
Islamia Girls' School, London

I Am An Artist

Art.
Art is printing the heart on a page
Sketching the imagination
Painting the words of my soul -
Art is me.

Art.
A call from the soul -
Desperately banging on the doors of society.
I want to be free -
From the corrupt grey stains that ordinary life leaves.
I want my soul to flow not be still -
My soul to dance miraculously
On top of the chains and bars and shackles.

Art.
The guardian angel -
Shielding me from the darkness and horror.
I want my art to kiss the world
And leave a permanent mark;
Without art
The world is bare, naked, empty.

Art.
Without it...
I am void of life,

Void of love, void of passion.
I am void.

I am nothing
If not an artist.

Siddiqah Maria Khan (15)
Islamia Girls' School, London

An Artist's Passion

My brush strokes the blank page,
The deep hues of paint seeping in
To the cold pressed paper with utmost rage,
Prussian blue and barium yellow,
Burnt sienna and bone white,
Just the sight makes my eyes tingle.

Although I am not Van Gogh or Da Vinci,
I promise I can make a fine art piece,
For hours on end with the time ticking,
Minutes go by, then hours, then days,
My pencils whimsically play on its canvas stage.

My passion for this may seem bizarre,
But now as my eyes lay upon the canvas,
No words can describe how I feel -
As the masterpiece I created kneels before me.

Maryam M Abdulrahman (16)
Islamia Girls' School, London

Summer

The happiness that I feel
When summer comes around.
I can't believe it's real
When I hear the bird sounds.

The plump fruits
And the birds chirping,
The flowers growing
And the seeds we are sowing.

But when the moon is sleeping,
The sun, so bright and gleaming,
Summer's beauty is shown in so many ways,
And Earth has never seen warmer days.

But when autumn arrives
And the bees go back to their beehives,
The feeling of joy is absent
And summer is not alive.

Amina Omer-Hashi (15)
Islamia Girls' School, London

Conflict

It started with one disagreement
And a difference of opinion...
The drawn-out line was starting to bend
As they let out all different kinds of emotion.
The tranquillity has already faded,
And the path we're going down is already paved.
Common sense has been locked away,
The anger and threats are all that stay.
The hope in this is already lost
And the price to pay is a huge weighty cost.

Zahira Khan (15)
Islamia Girls' School, London

Just Thinking

I've come to the realisation
That there is nothing in this world,
That there are only monsters created by creators
And creators created by monsters.

I've come to the realisation
That words like consequence are nonexistent
And that there are synonyms
Like achievement and praise as its replacement.

I've come to the realisation
That this world was created by mankind,
Yet mankind is the reason for no world.

I've come to the realisation
That it's ironic how we have options,
Yet we are unable to choose said option if needed,
That it's ironic how we have diversity,
Yet we are all afraid to be different.

Lottie Carpenter (15)
Ludlow CE School, Ludlow

Climate Change

Climate change
They're aware of it
Climate change
They choose to ignore it
Climate change
The wasting proceeds
Climate change
The consequences rise
Climate change
Burning
Melting
Killing
There really isn't any stopping
Not stopping their behaviour
Behaving in ways of selfishness or ignorance
Climate change
A disaster.

Esme Hodnett (13)
Ludlow CE School, Ludlow

The Gloomy Day

I looked around at the miserable sky.
Nothing to be seen but left to cry.

The atmosphere was filled with darkness...
Fulfilled with emotions and left heartless.

It is like a shadow over the world,
And I'm standing in the middle of the road.

Talha Mojid (12)
North West Surrey Short Stay School - Kingsway Centre, Woking

Left Out

I'm always the one who looks different
The one that says things wrong
The one who can't play certain games
Or sing that perfect song.

I'm the one that gets singled out
Whilst standing in a three
I'm the one who feels weird
When being the confusing me.

I'm the one with the weird thoughts
Circling my overcrowded brain
I'm the one who has to go over things
Again and again and again.

Yes I may look different
And speak different too
But that doesn't mean
I'm not human like you.

I picked up my pen this morning
Because I had a message to say
I need you to listen to me
For it is very important, okay?

Anybody who may be experiencing
The way I feel right now
Yes it may feel as painful
As a football foul.

Each of us are different
But there is no need to cower
Because it's what makes us different
That is our own superpower.

Etana-Rae Blake (12)
Outwood Academy City, Sheffield

Make The World Last

While we are enjoying Earth
It is coming to an end,
Think about all the animals and pets
That won't last to see the end,
The world is coming to an end,
Pollution is striking us the most,
The world is beaten up,
With floods to come with it,
The Antarctic ice is melting,
Going to the Earth's core,
While we are doing nothing
Except for making it worse,
Destroying our Earth's oxygen can
Like scuba diving in the Milky Way,
The world is coming to an end
And technology won't keep us to save us
While we're not helping.
So help us save the world
And make this world last forever,
Instead of striking it and seeing the end.
We can save the world,
And make it last,
So bring happiness and take care of the Earth,
And it will shelter us,
Smiling too.

Brandon Young (11)
Outwood Academy City, Sheffield

92

The Lunch

I was in school with my friends, walking down the corridor,
On my way to lunch.
Two minutes, three minutes, four minutes in the line.
When can we dine?
We step outside, sun blazing in our faces,
This is amazing, the weather was worthwhile waiting.
I sit down and continue to munch,
What time is it?
Oh, it's thirty minutes past one.
We continue to eat and talk as time passes by.
We get stares from everybody eye to eye.
The looks, the disgust, it is feeding on me.
I am scared. Confused. Worried about me.
This place, this earth,
It's full of weird stares.
Ignore them, focus on what actually cares.
The bell rang, we head upstairs
Like we don't care about the mean stares.
I am in lesson, it will not continue to be fair.
I must rest and end this poem right now and there.

Desiree Costa (11)
Outwood Academy City, Sheffield

My Planet

M y planet is where I like to be, my planet is a happy place for me!

Y ou may wonder, oh where is this planet? Now, let me tell you where you can find it.

P laced in the middle of your mind is your planet. Where you can let your thoughts go and your creative juices flow.

L iving your life is incredibly cool so why not live another one in your mind too?

A nyone can do it if they believe anything is possible and they can achieve.

N othing is impossible and nothing is unbelievable, it's all achievable.

E veryone has highs and lows even the best people and most successful in the world.

T his is what your planet is for, to keep those happy and amazing moments in your thoughts. So when you feel sad or upset just think of all those amazing moments instead.

Heidi McKay (11)
Outwood Academy City, Sheffield

Friends

Friends stick together with everything.
Go over to each other's houses and have fun.
You will know if they are a fake friend or a real friend
Because they will act differently to your real friends.
They will be mean or act off around you
So get rid of them and get real friends
Who will play and be happy and normal around you
But you may think that nobody likes you
Because they are fake friends
But don't think that because everyone wants to be friends
with you
Because you're kind-hearted and loving.
This is the meaning of friends.

F orever
R eal
I nclude you
E ncouraging
N ever give up
D etermined
S tay together.

Olivia Yates-Sykes (11)
Outwood Academy City, Sheffield

Pitch Invasion

On the field,
Playing football,
Chasing the football,
Pacing past the defenders.

All screaming my name,
The crowd going wild,
The last minute of the game,
Strike in the goal,
Goal!
Goal!
Goal!
All the people screaming my name.

Taming the away fans,
It was the day I sacrificed my life,
The day I will never look back on,
The day I will always remember,
The crowd was like the sound of a rattle.

Suddenly it went quiet
In a blink of an eye
Everyone screamed
"Pitch invasion!
Pitch invasion!"
As soon as you know
Everyone came running down towards the pitch.

Thanking God I scored
Because everyone loves me now.

Michaela Hopwood (11)
Outwood Academy City, Sheffield

The Dog

The day I will never forget
I hopped in my car with a face full of confusion
It was a sudden change
My parents were as silent as a mouse
Excited whispers, I couldn't hear,
Begging, persuading them to tell me where we were going
But I got no response
We quickly arrived at a house
We hurriedly jumped out of the car
My mother got me to knock on the door
They let us in
And my eyes fell on a family of dogs
Then I noticed
It all made sense
We were getting a dog
When my eyes lowered to the dog we were getting
I fell in love, like falling off a cliff
Welcome to the family, Sven.

Violet Berry (11)
Outwood Academy City, Sheffield

First Day Of School

I woke up early
Feeling all fresh and new
I put on my brand-new uniform
Worried about what I would do
Will I meet new people
Or make new friends?
Who will be my teachers
And will I even like them?
I slid on my shiny shoes
And picked up my bag
I walked out the door feeling happy but sad
I waved goodbye to my mum
Then set off in a flash
Step by step
I made my way to school
When I got there
I saw smiling teachers
With their arms open wide
Welcoming me in
Then at that point
I knew I was going to fit in.

Lily Hussain (12)
Outwood Academy City, Sheffield

The Sea

It glides, it shimmers, it rushes,
Through mounds of rocks,
But thrashes them to pieces until they're all gone.
The current flows with elegance and pride,
Its clear complexion also provides.
Its effects cause the share of light,
It glows but forms a key.
When it snows we need it the most
Yet it seems like no one cares.
No more cans!
The sea is not a wasteland!
So let's pick them up one by one.
The more we help, the more that's done.
It keeps us alive and helps us survive.
So let's make it thrive!

Khloe Shirley (11)
Outwood Academy City, Sheffield

School

I don't want to go to school,
I want to stay home and play games instead.
Teachers can be nice
But some make me want to stay in bed.
Don't get me started on the kids,
They make me want to growl and roar.
The food at school is not the best,
Sometimes it's so hard it could break your jaw.
Some subjects make me smile with glee,
Although PE makes me want to flee.
They say we need to be at school to learn
So that when we get a job we have lots to earn.

Finlay Wood (14)
Outwood Academy City, Sheffield

Covid-19

The first announcement,
Panic nationwide,
We couldn't even pronounce it,
It gave us quite a fright.

Thousands of cases,
Day by day,
People went to sleep
Not knowing if they would see light again.

I got the virus once,
The word couldn't be mentioned,
The word was Covid,
It had bad intentions.

Thousands of lives gone,
A vaccine that didn't even work,
Families six foot under,
Packed and covered with dirt.

Dylan Whitehead (13)
Outwood Academy City, Sheffield

The First Day

I remember the first day of secondary school
Worried and excited
Rushing to find the necessities
I made it to school
Now even more worried
I head inside the new school
I go to the hall
I get assigned a tutor group
Found out my best friend was three
Now I'm happy
I listen to the teacher
We get our assigned sets
Find out I have art
I'm now even happier
The end of the day comes
I leave school happy.

Summer Shaw (12)
Outwood Academy City, Sheffield

The One Day I Tried

That day in November, the 28th I recall,
The day started like an ordinary day.
I was walking down the street,
In the blink of an eye, a bird was in the road,
A car was coming,
I had no time to think,
Its wing got run over.

I ran over to the bird,
I picked it up as soon as I could.
Me and a couple of friends,
We kept the bird all day.
My friend said at least we tried today.
Then we took the bird to the vets.

Krystal Garner (11)
Outwood Academy City, Sheffield

The Lockdown

L oneliness stays upon me and belittles me

O nline with friends all night, playing Xbox

C atching the disease scared everyone

K indness was spreading through households

D epression filled people but not me

O ver the phone was laughter and a good time

W e always had a positive attitude to get away from a bad atmosphere

N ow everyone's back to normal but deep down I miss lockdown.

Loui Roberts (13)

Outwood Academy City, Sheffield

Lockdown Takes Over

Something rung,
No more normal life,
So what's happening now?
No seeing each other in person,
Only Zoom now.
That's not the same,
Can I go out?
Be normal?
It's the little things that matter,
Memories!
What if one day we all never wake up?
It's contagious now!
Outside! Outside!
That's all we know.
Hospitals, is it going to end?
Life just goes on and on.

Leah Grayson (13)
Outwood Academy City, Sheffield

Crimson Blood

The blood of not just our enemies
But also our comrades.
Not just the army men's blood,
It is also the blood of the people.
We have trained for this,
We must win this now.
For our comrades have fallen
To make us a bridge to victory.
Now this bridge is full of violence, pain,
Suffering and sadly death.
Too much death.
All our blood lies on the ground,
The trenches are our home.

Layton Lowe (11)
Outwood Academy City, Sheffield

Lockdown

L ove was lost, loneliness came.

O nward did the bad thoughts run through my brain.

C areless people, not following the law

K ind of made me angrier even more.

D eep down inside I actually felt calm.

O ther people felt so worried and alarmed.

W onderful memories were the things that mattered the most.

N ow I don't have to be a sad and lonely ghost.

Imogen Mugombe (13)

Outwood Academy City, Sheffield

The Night

The sun passes as I lay
I'm as quiet as a mouse
I think about my thoughts
As I fall to sleep
The rain taps on my window
The trees, swishing and turning side to side
Owls howl in their nests
I'm twisting and turning on my pillow
As I hear the autumn breeze
I feel sleepy as I think about the rain tapping on the window
And the next thing I know
I'm fast asleep in bed.

Grace Haythorne (11)
Outwood Academy City, Sheffield

My First Day Of School

I got out of bed
I felt like today was going to be dreadful
But a little bit of hope helped through the day
I got my pencil case full of pens, pencils and a ruler
But to make this cooler my favourite subjects are maths and PE
It was now the end of the day
School was great, I didn't need to worry
Now I go to bed and can't wait till tomorrow.

Luke Whyers (11)
Outwood Academy City, Sheffield

Pandemic

L oneliness haunted me.
O ut of touch with my family and friends.
C atching the disease, frightening everyone.
K ite flying without Nan and Grandad.
D isease, killing people like flies. Running
O ut of food in the shops.
W inter and Christmas without family.
N ausea, cold and sickness everywhere.

Zac Sylvester (13)

Outwood Academy City, Sheffield

Autumn Time

Autumn leaves
Red, gold and brown
Twirling and swirling
Drifting down

Prickly conkers
Cracking, popping
Branches snap
Acorns dropping

Picking pumpkins
Juicy apples too
Gathering blackberries
In hedgerows for you

Foggy mornings
Damp, cold and grey
Nature's blanket.

Tallulah Marples (11)
Outwood Academy City, Sheffield

The Stormy Night

The rain was pounding on the old and bumpy pavement,
The crash and smash as I was jumping with terror.
Lightning bolts were lighting up the sky,
Like my loving family.
But they were away,
And then an old rusty van like my mum's pulled in.
I screamed with joy... "Mum!"
I hugged her with excitement.

Kaiden Newall (12)
Outwood Academy City, Sheffield

Oh Air, Can't Wait Till I Get There!

There's no air
There's never any air
Imagine the air
The space has no air
Only home has air
The air, the air, can't wait till I get there,
Only if I had air I would be happy once again
Air, air, when will you come back to me?
Space is good
Without you it's nothing.

Maleek Kadir (11)
Outwood Academy City, Sheffield

Covid-19

L oneliness was the worst thing
O besity from nothing to do but eat
C reativity when you're bored
K illing themselves over depression
D ying of Covid
O nly playing games through lockdown
W orrying about family members
N o one to talk to.

Alfie King (13)

Outwood Academy City, Sheffield

Late Day

Yesterday I woke up late.
My mum yelled at me to get out of bed.
"Get up! Get changed!"
I looked at my phone, it was time for the farm.
I rushed to get my steel toecap boots.
My mum drove me to the farm,
I rapidly went to the feed room
To measure the feed and feed the animals.

Logan Parker (11)
Outwood Academy City, Sheffield

Lockdown

L oneliness getting out of hand
O ut of touch with family
C ooking food with only two ingredients
K nowing you could get it any minute
D epression coming and going
O ut of touch with friends
W hat could happen next?
N ow it is all over.

Jade Ledgerwood (13)
Outwood Academy City, Sheffield

Covid-19

Covid-19 is a new virus, spreading rapidly.
Covid - Hundreds of thousands of people left dead.
Corona - Thank goodness I can see my family again.
Oh no, back in lockdown with face masks, covid jabs.
Rona - Old people lonely, scared and wondering, *will I see daylight again?*

Jacob Ellis (13)
Outwood Academy City, Sheffield

Family

F amily is always the best
A nd they let your friends come as guests.
M y family is the best and all so sweet,
I love my family, they give me treats.
L oving your family isn't a test,
Y et you should always try your best.

Lucas Thompson (12)
Outwood Academy City, Sheffield

Lockdown

L ockdown was really tough
O besity took over
C ounting down the days
K ids bored at home
D ying from Covid
O verall the worst year
W orking from home
N o one can go out.

Chloe Tonks (13)
Outwood Academy City, Sheffield

You

Your touch is like the sun,
It warms the nights when we are together,
Yet on nights we are not I am cold and lonely.
On days we are together my face glows red, blush or
sunburn,
I do not mind for I will not regret a single moment I have
spent with you.
I love your touch.
Your eyes are like seas of blue crystals.
I could stare into them all day.
I do not blame the Titanic for going down in a sea as blue as
your eyes.
Your smile has me going on and on,
Your lips are so pretty I will kiss you every time I see them.
I love your smile.
Your voice is so pretty.
When you talk it comforts me,
I could listen forever.
I love your voice,
When you next hug me, never let go.
Next time you lock eyes with me, please don't look away.
Next time you kiss me, please don't ever pull away.
Next time you talk to me, know that I want to listen forever.
I will listen forever.
I love you, every part.
I will never let go of you, ever.

Lilly-May Pell (14)
Outwood Academy Normanby, Middlesbrough

God Save The Queen

The Georgian era is over
The Elizabethan times are here
A fresh young princess is now our Queen
A long and memorable reign begins.

War is still sharp in the nation's minds
It's time for a new beginning.

New inventions soar and spirits begin to lift
The boomers have started school
The polio vaccine is rolled out
The future is bright, no doubt.

We step into the sixties with new sounds and sight
All is not great for a small mining village
A sombre visit to Wales is high on the Queen's agenda
As time ticks by, a moon landing is a giant leap for mankind.

The sixties come to a close, decimalisation draws near
We turn from shillings to pence, let the confusion commence
Twenty-five years have passed, it's a milestone to celebrate
The Iron Lady makes her presence known.

Uncertain times roll in, the pits begin to close
Thousands of people protest, when it will end nobody knows
The Falklands need protecting
A new royal is married in with two princes following.

With the eighties left behind, flames spread through
Windsor Castle
Things are quickly changing, mourning the loss of a princess
As a new government is formed, things can only get better
Preparations for the new millennium begin for this once-in-a-
lifetime event.

Jubilee celebrations come to a halt with two tragedies just
weeks apart
Tearing apart Her Majesty's heart
But with air and grace, the Queen carries on
With no time to mourn, there's work to be done.

London hosts the Olympics
A secret agent returns
There's trouble brewing ahead
With Brexit and a lockdown, what more can be said?

The Queen's long reign is drawing to an end
Prince Philip passes on and leaves her all alone
But still there are celebrations to enjoy
A win for the women of England, and tea with a famous
bear.

It's been seventy years since the Georgian era, with parties
all around
Our Queen is looking tired, but there's one more job to be
done
Her fifteenth prime minister is invited round for tea
Little did we know it was the last of her we would see.

Her legacy will live on in hearts around the world
She will always be remembered
God save the Queen
Long live the King.

Grace Brown (12)
Outwood Academy Normanby, Middlesbrough

Friendship

F un times with your friends. From your favourite fun moments to funny jokes with your friends.

R elationships are key in friendship, a good friendship is having a good relationship.

I mportant. It's important to find a group of friends or friend that is a true friend. Kind and caring.

E ndless. Friendships that are true should never end. They won't want to leave you.

N ew friends. It's good to make new friends even if you have friends already.

D ifferent. It's good to be different from others, no one is the same.

S ometimes friends fall out, it happens to most friendships.

H elping your friends when they are sad or helping them finish their work and other things too.

I mportant. It's important that you like the friends you are with.

P erfect. Not all friendships are perfect but they don't have to be.

Honey Pattison (12)
Outwood Academy Normanby, Middlesbrough

Green To Grey

I presented my creation
A blessing to Earth
Although the earliest forms
Were hideous at birth.

I had trees, animals and seas
But that wasn't enough
I needed someone to care for me
To give me affection and love.

So I designed my product
I called them humans
They would develop me
Instead of leaving me in ruins.

They discovered the way of my planet
They gradually evolved
They built structures and had cultures
It can't go wrong, can it?

They evolved even more
I yelled, "Please stop!"
But my cries were engulfed
By the rise of plastic, it was everywhere in shops.

They forgot about me
They forgot about my needs
Oh, how foolish
Oh, take a glimpse. My degrees!

I felt myself becoming hot
The overwhelming stench of humid air, getting to my lungs
My species were dying and my sea levels were rising
I clenched my fist, I can't rely on anyone.

My oceans that used to shine like sapphire
Now dim and an enigmatic monster lives there
Just like plastic, constant sun has ruined something that
made me unique
My continent, Antarctica, left in despair, I wish this was
satire.

The concept of betrayal was so new to me
All I knew was how to be perfect
This world should resemble a fairy tale
You go through struggles,
But you always get a happy ending.

LilyMay Larsen (11)
Outwood Academy Normanby, Middlesbrough

Speak Up

I woke up in the night and heard my mum cry,
I felt sad and afraid but I wiped my tears dry.
There were times when I thought, *this can't be real*,
I prayed hard to God and we made a deal.
It was a shame the person making us sad
Was supposed to be my real dad.
Mum held us tight and took our hands,
We left in the night away from that man.
We left with nothing, we didn't have a home,
Me and my brother were brave, we didn't ever moan.
We were poor and hungry but Mum tried her best,
We asked for help and this was the test.
Ask for support, somebody will care,
Trust in others and they will be there.
There was a time when I felt I was blind, I couldn't see,
Then one day Mum surprised us with our new house key.
Be brave, have courage and you'll see one day,
That staying quiet about abuse is not okay.

Sophia Siraj (11)
Outwood Academy Normanby, Middlesbrough

A Horrible Nightmare

I was in a deep dream, I was nowhere I had ever seen,
Looking left there was a pack of alligators dying in a
polluted lake,
But they weren't alone, there was a very lonely drake.

Ten seconds later my location changed to a poor little polar
bear crying in pain.
He had been starving for days with no place to stay.
His house had melted and his food had swum away.

Once again my places changed.
I was in the middle of the sea
When a turtle came screaming for help as she couldn't
breathe.

Then I woke up feeling half dead.
It was 6am in the morning and a day ahead, full of dread.
This terrible dream came true,
All these poor animals were struggling to survive
When we think we're dying,
When we can't decide what to wear on the weekend.

Olivia Perry (11)
Outwood Academy Normanby, Middlesbrough

The Mind Of An Astronaut

My mind hesitated for a while as we floated through
darkness,
Skirting the craters' rims in the solar traffic - all waste;
Such unharnessed brightness from our bodies I never saw
on Earth -
White light, a joy, escaped from Geometer's cuticle
Into the clear uninhabited nothingness of space.

Drifting from planet to planet,
The gold of our light,
The gold spreading from the sheep's ear,
The gold out of our light into moronic space,
Gold as it is, itself, leaf of gold,
Shattered in the distance as the winds heard,
Our preoccupation with gold,
Forgetting the desiccating diaphragm,
Gold, such as it is, on our planet, on another in space with
us.
Our heads made of white gold,
Our hearts of gilt, our souls waste away;
That's my mind.

Elexie Lynes (12)
Outwood Academy Normanby, Middlesbrough

My Huge Chocolate Bar

Whose chocolate is that?
I think I might know.
Its owner is quite happy though.
Full of joy, like a shiny rainbow,
I watch him say 'yum'.
I cry hello.
He gives his chocolate a shake,
And laughs until his belly aches.
The only other sound is the break,
With distant noises and birds awake.
The chocolate is massive, delicious and deep,
But he has promises to keep,
He rises from his super-soft bed
With thoughts of chocolate in his head.
He wakes and eats his bread with lots of chocolate spread
Ready for the day ahead.
It is easily his favourite thing by far,
His huge and delicious chocolate bar.

Ollie McGarry (12)
Outwood Academy Normanby, Middlesbrough

Hero

When I was nine
Tom Fletcher gave me a sign
That all I needed was books.
'The Creakers' left me on the hooks.

When I was ten
Julia Donaldson made me not want to go back again.
'The Gruffalo' and 'What the Ladybird Heard' caused me to write my own word.

When I was eleven
J K Rowling's books were like adventure and fantasy heaven.
'The Philosopher's Stone' was obviously the first one I read.

Now I'm twelve
Alice Osman's books just excel -
'The Heartstopper' series left people beheld.
The novels made people come up with a lot of theories.

Bethany Quinn (12)
Outwood Academy Normanby, Middlesbrough

Ode To The Fish

My happy fish, you inspire me to write.
I hate the way you feed, waddle and flap,
Invading my mind day and through the night,
Always dreaming about the pleasant lap.

Let me compare you to a non-member?
You are more mighty, unhappy and soft,
Weak fog hides the oceans of November,
And autumn time has the almighty waft.

How do I hate you? Let me count the ways.
I hate your unpleasant feet, smile and thumb.
Thinking of your flappy smile fills my days.
My hate for you is the Jamaican rum.

Now I must away with a happy heart,
Remember my big words whilst we're apart.

Liam Daniels (12)
Outwood Academy Normanby, Middlesbrough

Sweets, Glorious Sweets

Sweets are scrummy,
Sweets are lovely.
They are round,
They are thin.
Sweets are chewy,
Sweets are solid.

These are colourful,
They are vibrant
And many sizes.
Some chocolates,
Some jellies,
Some even like big bellies.
Sweets are heaven,
If you like them.

Sweets are a land of favourite things,
Sweets are a cosy teddy bear.
They make people happy when they are miserable
And are like a big bottle of Ribena for adults.

Sweets are a door
To the land of joy.
They are bought in shops
Where people plan plots.

Tanisha Sellars (11)
Outwood Academy Normanby, Middlesbrough

Love Is Forever

Roses are red, violets are blue
I can't express my feelings for you.
I love you to the moon and back
And even far away you will be in my mind.
My heart be pounding like never before,
And I can't control my love for you anymore.
Leaves be falling from trees
And we be fighting like two lovebirds in a pear tree.
But our bond is forever
No matter how far or close we are together.
Love is forever no matter what
And when our time is at an end
We will remember the good, happy times we spent together.
Love is forever.

Faith McGarry (13)
Outwood Academy Normanby, Middlesbrough

Silent Street

The street was silent,
It is normally quite violent.
Dogs would play,
Even with a stray.
But not a sound could be heard,
Not a whisper, not a word.

The street was silent,
It is normally quite violent.
Cars would blare their horn,
And my ears would be torn.
The noise on the street belongs
But not a stumble or even some sing-alongs.

The street was silent,
It is normally quite violent.
Children would argue,
Down the venue.
Not a bark,
In the dark.

Layla-Rose Spence (12)
Outwood Academy Normanby, Middlesbrough

Where The Cherry Blossom Falls

We are expected
To look like winter
Bare, bleak and small
As the days are short
Not a morsel of fat
To keep us warm.

I treasure my blossom
But she shall grow and bloom
Our bodies change
Like the seasons
And our real beauty
Comes out at spring.

When blossoms touch our cheeks
Stretch marks flourish
Like flowering vines
We bloom into ourselves
And the fleeting nature of life
Where the cherry blossom falls.

Millie Brown (12)
Outwood Academy Normanby, Middlesbrough

Never Give Up

Never give up, it's not always just luck
Remember to give it a try
Even if you are feeling low or high
If you get it wrong first time
Always put yourself back in line
If you feel like you're never gonna get it right
Try again and put up a fight

Resilience is the key
Even if it's tricky
Always try again
It's never quite the end

Winners never quit
Quitters never win
The rule is to never give in.

Nancy Brookes (11)
Outwood Academy Normanby, Middlesbrough

Midnight

Lying awake at midnight,
Morning was one to excite,
Brain still racing,
Trying to stop it pacing.

Thought after thought,
Attempting to get them to nought,
Worrying what might happen next,
Feeling very perplexed.

Wishing the night away,
Getting ready for the next day,
Hoping to plan every step,
Even though I haven't slept.

Lying awake at midnight,
Waiting for the daylight.

Emily Mcroy (14)
Outwood Academy Normanby, Middlesbrough

Family

To be in a family like mine is so divine.
They are the first to know you
And are the ones who gave you your name.
Cherish them while you have them
Before it's too late.
As you know family is everything.
Families come together for always and forever,
Any time, any season.
Family is more important than going to work or friends,
It's about spending time together.
A family is a gift that is never unwrapped.

Lacee Thompson (11)
Outwood Academy Normanby, Middlesbrough

Spring Poem

As the sun starts to rise
Everyone starts to open their eyes.
The flowers start to bloom
And caterpillars spin their cocoons.
Animals are being born
And some people are cutting the lawn.
Dogs are playing fetch
As babies start to stretch.
Picnics are beginning to appear
And people are strolling down the pier.
As the end of the day grows near
Everyone starts to clear.

Riley Henderson (11)
Outwood Academy Normanby, Middlesbrough

Rid The World Of Bullies

"Bullying has to stop,"
Most people say.
But others like to cause pain
Like harsh rain,
Brought to hurt.

Words, words,
So strong they are.
They hurt so many,
So bad
Every day.

Nowhere can we escape
From the harsh rain.
But in the breeze, in the trees
We find the kind.
They say,
"Rid the world of bullies!"

Willow Rose Thompson (11)
Outwood Academy Normanby, Middlesbrough

The Extraordinary Environment

From the plains of Africa,
To the icy desert of Antarctica,
The world is beautiful inside and out.
Don't hurt the world,
The world is so nice.
If you are going to,
Please think twice.

Charlie Hanley (11)
Outwood Academy Normanby, Middlesbrough

Horrific Pollution

There's no point in asking,
No point even trying,
It doesn't matter, don't listen,
It's only our Earth that is dying!

All of the animals
That live in the hedge,
They are now endangered:
Living on the edge.

You may worry
They say, "We are all good,"
But think of all those places
Flushing with floods.

"Let's look on the bright side!
No need to worry,"
But all the Earth's problems
Shall come in a flurry.

"But how? But when?"
"What's the solution?"
"How will we end
This horrific pollution?"

We'll start with the small things.
"But when will it be done?"
Not sure, but remember,
We will unite as one!

Eve Cox (11)

Serlby Park Academy, Bircotes

What A Wonderful World (Not!)

What do coral reefs do,
Down in the deep, deep blue?

It's home to all the tropical fish,
Forever will be there I wish.

All of the plastic that goes in the sea
Will go in the fish and then into me.

The icebergs so tall, pointing to the sky,
Will slowly melt down and soon start to die!

Why is this happening to our once-perfect Earth?
What are we doing? What is it worth?

Together we can change this, at least we can try,
If we don't soon then our planet will die!

Hayden Squire (11)
Serlby Park Academy, Bircotes

We're Destroying Our Earth

We're destroying our Earth,
It's not at all fun.
The animals are dying,
Look at what we have done.
Forest fires are destroying homes,
Destroying the places that they love the most.
Chemicals are slowly filling our air,
Icebergs are melting and we don't even care.
Take a moment to think why we did all of this.
Was it to help the Earth or for our own benefit?
I was thinking about this late one night,
If the old world saw this would it give them a fright?
That we destroyed so much of their precious land,
We're killing the forest, the snow and the sand.
The old world would ask, "Where have the animals gone?"
We'd say, "We don't know as they've been gone for so long."
Old us would cry over what we have done.
We're destroying our Earth
And it's not at all fun.

Allegra Cesar (12)
St George's College Weybridge, Addlestone

Leading To The Future

Have you seen the look on my face?
...What an utter disgrace,
What a waste we've been making,
All the plastic we're taking,

We throw it away,
It washes a bay,
All the money we're spending,
And the rules we are bending,
We're cutting down trees,
With way too much ease!
Don't you feel bad?
I think we've gone mad!
What about our poor ocean?
And our lack of devotion?
This disaster is not fair,
So get out there, take action,
To all our satisfaction,
Anger is rising,
Our time is minimising,

Why don't we repair?
This just isn't fair!
We've got to reduce,
The amount of plastic use,
Think about reusing,

Or I'll continue accusing,
And last but not least,
Remember to recycle!

What's right is right,
So lead to the light!
Let your voice speak out,
That's what confidence is about.
Speak big and loud,
Don't be a coward!
You could try to be fitter by picking up litter,
But instead we are keen to continue being mean!
Let's change our attitude,
And show the Earth our gratitude!

Mila Elahi (11)
St George's College Weybridge, Addlestone

I'm Sorry World

There are no more highlights of white in the golden, peach sky.
No more time for people to lie,
That there are still stars shining bright
In the dark, endless night.

Instead, smoke crawls up each cloud,
Not doing the birds proud.

The dusk-bruised sky
Always makes me cry.
Tears fall through the cracks of a broken Earth
As I think of all that we took in our path.

Our world is broken,
Abandoned, deserted and unspoken.
We all stopped praising,
And starting derailing.

Pollution weaves through the air
But we don't seem to care.
We say our Earth is our foe,
But can we really not see and know?

It is us!
We broke the trust!
We started the war of the coal-black clouds!
We are the ones who broke the vows.

Those plastic bags make us feel relieved
But the world feels so very deceived.
Earth's apples are dimes
But we steal them and commit so many crimes!

I just want to say, I'm sorry world,
I promise the truth will soon unfold!

Maya Pozina (12)
St George's College Weybridge, Addlestone

There's One Star

There's one star I used to always see,
It would open me up as if I was a door and it was a key,
It relieved all my stress
As if I was wearing a flowery dress.
My flower blooms
But the skyscraper still looms.
I want to scream like a rocket, *boom, boom, boom!*

There was always one bee
Now he's stuck with a plea,
"I try to take care with all I do,
But I'm stuck with people like you,
I want to help
But all I can do is yelp,
There's now too much powder
And you're taking away all my power."

A piece of our Earth
Is cracking on the hearth,
We're watching it die
As all we do is sit there and lie.
The TV screen
Is trying to scream,
It hears all we say
And wants to cry every day

'Cause it knows we're wrong,
We can't be saved by King Kong!

There's one star I used to always see,
But now it's locked away
'Cause we've destroyed the key.

Scout Westen (12)
St George's College Weybridge, Addlestone

Endangered Animals

These animals fall like flies,
Throughout the day and night.
One has gone, two have gone,
Then suddenly 1,000 have gone.
Why do these animals
Have to die because of stupid things humans do?
They are like us,
They have fun, they hurt, they play, they cry.
Why do we have to hurt them?
When one falls,
They all fall.
They feel,
They understand.
They live.
Our planet needs us to help it,
Not destroy it.
Animals are part of this world,
They are a part of our wide community.
We should build that community,
Not slowly shrink it.
Imagine a world with no tigers,
Or all the tiny, colourful, miraculous butterflies.
Or the sea creatures that lurk under the surface,
Like intelligent whales that can sing like angels.

Who would want to destroy this harmony we live in?
Don't get rid of animals,
Help them grow!

Alice Dines (11)

St George's College Weybridge, Addlestone

Stranger Things

Season one was a blast
Will escaped pretty fast
Barb disappeared when she was wet
Nancy found out and got pretty upset
That's when the group met Eleven
She had been hiding 24/7
Eggo waffles taste like heaven.

Season two was exciting
Eleven is tired of hiding
Will thinks he's in the Upside Down
It's the curse of Hawkins' town.

Season three was pretty cool
Mind Flayer showed up in Starcourt mall
Will's haircut was still a bowl
Although Billy was hard to control
He sacrificed his life for Eleven
Woah!

Season four was full of Kate Bush
Killing Vecna was quite a rush
No one is afraid of the Upside Down
Eddie's death made us all frown.

Season five isn't coming for ages
This show's so good it has multiple stages.

Frank Challouma (11)
St George's College Weybridge, Addlestone

World War Christmas

'Twas the night of Christmas Eve,
It was a dark time.
Germany was under Hitler's rule,
Hiding in ditches we were waiting for light,
You cannot fight wars in the middle of the night.

It was cold and damp, we were all tired,
But we couldn't give up in case the Germans fired.
The guns shouted and roared,
The bombs with flames like a sword.

Brave friends of mine fought in Christmas air,
Sadly, no Santa was there.
We dream of home and those we love,
We dream of them in the skies above.

There was no need for death,
Just to get power.
Hopefully one day our memory will be remembered,
Through these sweet red flowers.

Ted Langrish (11)
St George's College Weybridge, Addlestone

Solution To Pollution

Pollution is a problem in need of a solution,
but all this plastic in the sea really upsets me.
While this ocean is being destroyed we feel no emotion,
but 160,000 million fish are being killed every second,
nobody reckons that it matters but plastic is working its way
up the food chain,
into our stomach and causing us pain.
Sea creatures die and become toxic,
whilst we sit at home, watch clocks tick.
We need to act fast to make this devastation
a thing of the past.
Think about what you put on your plate,
before it's too late.
This is why we need to find a solution to this horrible
problem known as plastic pollution.

Jessica Rolton (11)
St George's College Weybridge, Addlestone

Our World Is Too Late

Work is nothing but a charade,
Our world is dying, workers go underpaid.
98% of what you learn is a waste.
But it's okay, it's all fine,
It won't break down on a dime.
Oh no... I forgot the next line.
No! It's not fine, we're great?
These words are fake,
Our Earth still shakes.
Trees are on fire,
Let's get them some water so they don't bake.
Don't worry it'll be fine
It'll all improve,
Let's do some more to improve the mood.
This isn't true,
With that attitude, our world will continue to quake.
What more can we do?
Our world is too late.

Finlay Bolah (12)
St George's College Weybridge, Addlestone

Pigeon

How does anyone know how it feels,
To be a nuisance to all humankind,
Being chased around aimlessly,
And everyone forgets we are one of a kind?

The majority of them
Think we just make a mess.
Everyone forgets how we helped in the war,
Delivering messages to every foreign address.

Most of us have been hurt,
Bullied, driven out of our minds!
You don't abuse other animals,
Our ancestors were so loyal and wise.

Now we vow our coo shall be heard,
Those of us who suffered to be avenged,
Please change the way you treat us,
Or we solemnly swear we'll get revenge!

Alexia Mattina (12)
St George's College Weybridge, Addlestone

Our World

This is our world,
The only Earth,
We have to protect it,
Before it's too late.

Arctic ice is melting,
Polar bears losing their homes,
The frozen lands are thawing,
Making sea levels rise.

Rainforests decreasing by the minute,
Farms replacing ground where rainforests used to thrive,
Animals dying as quickly as the trees,
Nature is being defeated by greed.

Cars releasing dirty fumes,
Industry smoke fills the sky,
Oxygen consumed, carbon released
Causing global temperatures to soar.

One world,
One chance,
To change,
No time.

Emma Muraszko (11)
St George's College Weybridge, Addlestone

The Environment

The environment is dying, we need to play our role,
Everything and anything, even saving a singular mole.
Putting in the effort could really save the planet,
If not then next on the list is a gannet.

Trees getting cut down every single minute,
When we see a plastic bag we have to bin it.
Water levels rising, we have to lower the heat,
Using cows for food isn't efficient meat.

Losing habitats, killing animals' homes,
Taking away everything, even the kings on their thrones.
Fuels are depleting, we have to switch energy!
After 2100 nothing but the earth!

Thomas Wolf (12)
St George's College Weybridge, Addlestone

Global Warming

The Earth is dying and no one is trying,
Glaciers are melting, the trees are crying,
I want to go back to the world we knew,
All those animals, now there's only a few,
Air pollution is rife, factories won't stop,
Rainforest, mountains and sand, they all might flop,
In summer it's cold but in winter it's hot,
Global warming can't understand what is what,
Litter in oceans, we went from green to black,
If we want to save our Earth we're not on track,
Cities and buildings are getting way too much,
Respect our nature before I hold a crutch.

Amy Cotterell (12)
St George's College Weybridge, Addlestone

Animals Do Matter

Animals have rights like humans
Because we are animals too.
Their lives do matter.
They have feelings like me and you.

If only we lived in a world
Where animals are treated fairly
They aren't used as circus toys
And humans kill them rarely.

A lion shouldn't starve to death
A leopard shouldn't be scared
An elephant isn't your new horse
A giraffe's tail shouldn't have to be repaired.

Now we need to work together
To make animals feel safe
We need to stop extinction
It still isn't too late.

Siena Lenman (11)
St George's College Weybridge, Addlestone

Nature

I need to tell you about deforestation
Next time you go to work, walk, don't go to the train station
Everywhere trees are getting cut down
When I see global warming it gives me a frown
Every second sea creatures are losing their homes
Kings of the jungle, losing their thrones
All around the world pollution is filling the air
The way all animals are living isn't fair
Icebergs are melting everywhere
We need to comfort and help the penguins and the polar bears
Trees are getting cut down every single minute
If we see a plastic bag we have to bin it.

Ben Puddephatt (12)
St George's College Weybridge, Addlestone

Endangered Environment

We need to save the environment, it's luscious and green,
It's getting polluted, let's keep the Earth clean.
So much junk I can see,
What if the Earth was clean?

Water, stream, flowing forever,
All types of water, animals bunched together.
Multiple insects in the heather,
Fish swimming into bottles,
They aren't that clever.

Trees always falling down,
Cars, aeroplanes, harming the planet,
Revving their engines, creating sound,
People hogging the fuel like a gannet.

Please let's save the environment!

Max Brindley (11)
St George's College Weybridge, Addlestone

Save The Animals

We're killing animals, don't you care?
And some of these animals are really quite rare.
They're going extinct, they're all going to die.
I know you do care and don't try to lie.
So that's where I'll leave you,
Yes, that's what I'll do
I'll leave you some time, a couple of days
Or maybe just as long as it takes
For you to decide what you're going to do.
Yes of course, I'm talking to you!
To help save the animals that live in this world,
This wonderful world,
The animals that live in this world.

Juliana Lima (11)
St George's College Weybridge, Addlestone

The Environment

The ice is melting and no one helping
The penguins and polar bears are shouting and yelping
The trees are being cut down short
And more plastic is being bought
More and more is thrown in the ocean
And to save it, we need to take motion
Poisonous gases are flooding the air
The way we treat the planet is really not fair
Fires are starting left, right and centre
Help save the planet or more will enter
Coral reefs keep going dim
Because of the harm that we let in
Help save the planet in any way
Help save the planet, and try today.

Sophia Jory (12)
St George's College Weybridge, Addlestone

Environment

E veryone needs to protect the planet.

N ow the world is suffering and dying.

V ery big population and so much pollution.

I believe we should look after the planet and not destroy it.

R esponsibility! Our responsibility! This is our responsibility!

O nly we can change the world.

N ow the world is suffering and dying

M any trees are dying, many people are crying.

E very polar bear is dying.

N ow koalas are crying, every plant is dying.

T rees are green and we should be too!

Sammy Hooper (11)

St George's College Weybridge, Addlestone

The Environment, My Environment

The environment, don't you love it too?
Trees, leaves, greenhouses, don't you love it too?
Trashed turtles, wrapped seagulls, do we really want this?
I hate it, just hate it when you hear on the news
About all of the animals with all their sad blues.
But when you hear about the good news too
It feels too good to be true
When they find the cutest animals,
And make the forests anti-flammable.
So if you are like me
And you really like the trees,
Try your best to help us
And keep the world clean.

Ben Fellows (11)
St George's College Weybridge, Addlestone

So Why?

Climate change
We all know it
So why haven't we changed?
The world is getting damaged
It can no longer manage
So why haven't we changed?
Some say we have
But our actions are yet to be arranged
So why haven't we changed?
Animals are dying
Sea levels are rising
So why haven't we changed?
Littering is taking place
Destroying the precious green space
So why haven't we changed?
If we don't respond to this fear
Our world will disappear
So we better change.

Tobiah Eldridge (12)
St George's College Weybridge, Addlestone

Our Environment

Our environment is being damaged endlessly,
So we must protect it and make sure it does not get worse.
Deforestation is no joke,
So don't mock it and act as if it is not your problem.
Don't pity those who take all the damage,
Try to make a change for their benefit.
Think about recycling
Because if you don't it shall bite back at you.
Don't cut down trees that are in the way,
It's not their fault that they ended up where they did.
Try to remember this poem,
In order to save the world.

Filip Matejka (11)
St George's College Weybridge, Addlestone

I Hate Litter

Would you let someone throw litter in your bed?
But you think it's okay to throw it in the forest instead
The forest is lovely
The forest is free
But litter is making it dingy and bleak.

People are mean
Dropping litter amongst the trees
The forest is a home
A home to living things.

I hate litter
It's a wretched thing
Rubbish never leaves
And it ruins a beautiful thing.

I hate litter
So let's be clear
It's evil
And should be illegal.

Beth Harrison (12)
St George's College Weybridge, Addlestone

Landfill

Landfill, row upon row, pile upon pile,
Trash covering our Earth for mile upon mile.
It's on our land and it's in our seas,
Our dear Mother Nature is begging on her knees.

Our wildlife is suffering from extinction.

Trees are falling to the ground.
As they topple you hear the earth pound.
Fires are burning, tearing through the trees,
The fire roars as anything living flees.

Our Earth is sending us calls for help
But everyone will ignore it until it cries and it yelps.

Aidan Geraghty (12)
St George's College Weybridge, Addlestone

Stop Animal Endangerment

These poor, loving animals have no home,
They have been abandoned, left alone.
I want to go back to the old world,
Everything here has been hurled.
We've put our animals in so much danger,
Why's everyone acting like a stranger?
We need to save them as soon as we can,
Using their fur as a sofa or a fan.
Animals are dying and no one is trying,
Cats in trees, puppies crying.
How can someone say this with a good tone,
The kings of the jungles are losing their thrones.

Bonnie Young (13)
St George's College Weybridge, Addlestone

I Love Animals, Don't You?

I love animals, don't you?
They're different from us, they're something new
So you tell me why are people so cruel?
They destroy their homes and families too.

I love animals, don't you?
All different shapes and sizes too
So you tell me, can't we act?
We're the equivalent of a pack
If we collaborate we can change the sphere
From dark and empty to bright and full
So come with me and change the world.

I love animals, don't you?

Johanna Martius-Jones (11)
St George's College Weybridge, Addlestone

Deforestation

Deforestation isn't a joke,
What will happen to those jungle-living folk?
Don't cut down the trees,
What about the animals, the bees?
Because of you, the rainforests are destroyed
And people like me are getting annoyed.
You are currently wiping out all wildlife,
The axe that you chop with is sharper than a knife.
A change must be made
Or the next generation's future will fade.
So do something now.
To get out of this chaos you have to think, *how?*

Ishwer Najjhur (11)
St George's College Weybridge, Addlestone

Earth's Personal Loss

The last time I saw Papa was on my birthday.
I was too afraid to say goodbye.
A few days later, I learnt he had gone.
But now I know he is one with the Earth.

We all are.

And if we all are one with this world,
Why do we mistreat it so?
And if our loved ones are one with the Earth,
Why do we mistreat it so?

I'll leave you with this question,
And maybe soon you'll see
Why, why, why
Why we should not treat it so?

Enid Howes Barley (11)
St George's College Weybridge, Addlestone

Monkey Fire

Monkey swinging from vine to vine
Engulfed in flames, blazing to shine
Streaks of blood ready to slay
I shall not live to see another day.

I was thinking you could be trusted
Ashes in the wound now it's all rusted
Wretched rage wrecking the wood
Fertile, fair, now broken, you should...

Blades shrieking in the air
My life is hatred, wish it was fair
Monkey swinging from vine to vine
Your life is happy, dull with death is mine.

James Pittard (11)
St George's College Weybridge, Addlestone

The Environment

Just look what we're doing,
Our world, crumbling every day,
Our planet is important,
So let's treat it the right way.

Birds flying high in the sky
Or sitting on branches,
Let's hope they don't die.

Think about coal mining,
Releasing smoke in the air,
Why do we need this?
There are trees everywhere.

Lands of deforestation,
So far and wide,
Animals losing their homes,
Just trying to hide.

Emily Wainwright (11)
St George's College Weybridge, Addlestone

Our World

The birds and the bees
The plants, flowers and green trees
They make up our world.

But there are issues
With the way we care for it.
A few examples:

Deforestation.
Trees are called 'lungs of the Earth'.
They're cut down. Earth dies.

Illegal poaching.
Wildlife, killed because of greed.
Innocent life, slain.

Our world is dying
And it's all because of us.

What are we doing?

Emma Lee (12)
St George's College Weybridge, Addlestone

I Loved The Sea

I love the sea
But not how it is now
I liked it when it was free
Free of oils, plastic and debris.

I loved the sea
For its aqua blue waters
Full of living things unseen
For its surface which was clean.

But I think we can help
We can help wipe our seas clean
Because now we hear it yelp
We should save everything, even the kelp.

So now all join me
In cleaning the sea
I hope to make many more memories.

Isobel Bokenham (12)
St George's College Weybridge, Addlestone

Society

Society anxiety...
Why does it feel like everyone is judging me?
'Cause when I walk past you and you look me in the eyes,
I feel a shiver go down my spine
And I pretend that I'm alright
And everything in my head is jumbling and racing,
But I can't tell anyone because I'm scared they'll think I'm faking.
This society is built for anxiety,
Do you think only I'm failing?
Because I think this whole world is decaying.

Florence Langlands (11)
St George's College Weybridge, Addlestone

America, America, What Lovely America

America, America, what lovely America.
The crystal-clear sea, what else could you ask for?
It is as spectacular as a dream!
The sunset lay upon your eyes as if the colours of the world have reignited.

America, America, what lovely America.
The luscious green grass sprawled upon acres.
Tall, towering trees spread out in every possible space to be grown.
It inspired me to be who I am now.
Help to keep the environment like it is.

Sebastian Edwards (11)
St George's College Weybridge, Addlestone

They Are Just Like Us

Animals, the first species of the Earth,
They eat,
They love,
They laugh and cry
And they mourn with sadness and grief.
They are just like us
But what do we do?
We are driving
And thriving
And sending them away
But then we find them washed up on the bays
Alone
But we still chuck things in the ocean
Which puts animals under a potion
Until there is none left.
They are just like us.

Gabriella Hern (12)
St George's College Weybridge, Addlestone

I Hate All Plastic Bags

I hate all plastic bags
'Cause they make baby turtles sad
By killing all their mums and dads.

I hate all plastic bags
'Cause they are killing all the crabs
This makes me very sad.

Why do we use plastic bags
When we know they are killing crabs
And making baby turtles sad?

We know this is very bad
We know we are making turtles sad
But we still buy plastic bags.

Oscar Ryan (12)
St George's College Weybridge, Addlestone

Night Falls

When night falls, do you hear whispers?
The dead trying to say that you should be ready...
Ready for what comes next...
The silence is ear-breaking, the darkness absolute...

What was that?
The void-like sky terrified me
I was idle
Like a statue.

There was a rustle in the bush
My soul was slowly and painfully... cracking
That's why
I don't go out when night falls.

Jacques Marais (11)
St George's College Weybridge, Addlestone

The World Around Us

Trees are falling down everywhere
Litter in the ocean
Animals are being stripped from their homes
Our world is falling apart
Torn by anger and misery
We need to change our ways of life
Or life itself will end.

Nature is dying all around
And I am dying inside
For if we don't stop
The world we know will disappear.

We need to act before it's too late.

Emilia Bownds (11)
St George's College Weybridge, Addlestone

Barbados

Barbados, palm trees swaying in the wind
Whilst the sea splatters and flings
The sea is warm and full of creatures
And lots of wonderful features
They try to keep it clean
But not everyone is keen
Turtles in the sea want to swim freely
Beaches are still better than ever, luckily
Plants are starting to take back what's theirs
Their land and their waters.

Katie-Mae Hogg (11)
St George's College Weybridge, Addlestone

The Problem

The problem's unspoken,
As we are making our planet broken.
Icebergs are melting,
We are infecting our air,
Get up from your chair,
And show that you care.
We need to be more green
'Cause people are being too mean.
There aren't enough bees,
Stop knocking down trees.
So now the problem's spoken,
Can we make our planet un-broken?

Jessica Hooper (12)
St George's College Weybridge, Addlestone

Green Energy

Resources and materials are being misused,
Most ways of creating it is by making fumes,
But there is a way of ending our doom,
By using sustainable energy there will be a lot less fumes for
the atmosphere to consume,
Gas is spreading around the atmosphere like the flu,
We can make a difference to stop the gloom,
So let's use sustainable energy to save me and you.

Jasper Gill (12)
St George's College Weybridge, Addlestone

Stop Cutting Down Trees

Stop cutting down trees!
Without them the Earth is falling to its knees.
Trees keep us alive,
Buzzing like bees in a beehive.

Trees are so green,
So how can we be so mean?
Trees, trees, trees,
Guardians of the Earth.

They are kings of the rainforest,
Standing so tall,
One thing we need to do
Is stop cutting down the trees!

Connor Duckworth (12)
St George's College Weybridge, Addlestone

Why Are We Destroying Nature?

Nature is fading
Bang!
Another tree is gone
Bang!
Another animal's home is gone
Bang!
Another life is gone
Our nature is fading
The trees, standing tall, keeping us safe
Giving all of us life
The flowers, popping with colour
Brightening up the world
And all we are doing
is destroying it.

Benjamin Kay (12)
St George's College Weybridge, Addlestone

My Rainforest Haiku Poem

The wild rainforest
The amazing Amazon
The poison dart frogs.

Amazon river
With lots of inhabitants
Fish, birds and monkeys.

Protect our jungles
To save all our animals
And plants in our world.

Our world is special
We need to look after it
So please do your bit

To help save our planet.

Louis Bortnik (11)
St George's College Weybridge, Addlestone

They All Kept Going

They don't like the way she talks
or the way she walks,
they don't like the way he looks
or the way he cooks,
they don't like the clothes they wear
or the thoughts he shares.

But neither he, she, or they care!
None of them stopped moving on,
none of them let the things they said stop them.

Sofia Stotter-Brooks (12)
St George's College Weybridge, Addlestone

Nature

I like the green, lush leaves
And the things that trees want to achieve.
You can climb a tree
And wait for a beautiful thing to see.

I don't like stinging nettles,
They don't look beautiful and they don't have petals.
I remember when I fell into loads of nettles
And stings started to settle.

Oscar Sibley (11)
St George's College Weybridge, Addlestone

The Sounds Of Basketball

The squeak of sneakers
The pounding of feet
The sounds on the courts
Are just so sweet
The dribble of balls
And my teammate calls
Every cheer
Brings happiness to my ears
There are many sounds
But the one I like the best
Is probably the swish
Of the ball going through the net.

George Davis (11)

St George's College Weybridge, Addlestone

What Is Life?

What is life? Well.
Life can be a story that we write.
Life could be a picture,
a picture that we paint.
But what is the meaning of life?
Life is a number,
a number that we choose.

Life is a wish, a wish upon a star.

Life to me is freedom.
Freedom we must take.

Tessa Gerber (11)
St George's College Weybridge, Addlestone

Trees

Trees, they are so cool
Who would be such a fool to cut trees down?
Trees can be the most beautiful things on the planet.
Oh damn it!
Why do people cut down trees?

Mark Morcos (11)
St George's College Weybridge, Addlestone

Trees

Green, green, green...
The trees sit
Brown, brown, brown...
The trees lie
Trees, trees, trees...
The trees die.

Rory Hotchkiss (13)
St George's College Weybridge, Addlestone

Lost

You've never ever felt this way,
Until you had to say goodbye.
The sort of pain you have to go through,
It's like committing suicide.
You can't focus, you're tired,
Their face is all your mind can see.
Your chest is so tight that sometimes it's impossible to breathe.
"It's impossible, there's no way you can ever meet them,"
your friend said.
Unless I do suicide, just to be with them
Just carrying on as normal feels like you're saying 'I don't even care',
But you don't even know what you're going to do,
God, this isn't fair!
You've been told you need to get through this,
That things get easier in time
But it's the worst feeling you've ever felt
To actually be the one who's left behind.
Now don't go and think further,
Come and listen here...
No matter how many people you may lose
You have no choice but to go on living, my dear.
No matter how devastating the blows may be,
They will always still be near.

Aryanna Madzura (11)
St Patrick's RC High School & Arts College, Eccles

Black Is My Superpower

Why do I not look like the other girls?
Am I pretty enough?
You may be pretty but you're just not white.
Just face it, that's what life will always be.
Living in the shadows of a white girl.
We are portrayed as ugly,
That's why Barbie ain't black.
I look back and I think, *why wasn't Barbie black?*
We've been brought up to be hated, eradicated.
Who am I to think I can change the world
When I'm nothing but a black girl?
I was ashamed of my hair,
Ashamed of my culture,
Ashamed to live as a woman of colour.
The burden I carry, the guilt I bring,
The wanting of love, the wanting of change.
We can't let another generation be indoctrinated,
Manipulated, segregated, discriminated.
What is beauty?
Beauty is me and beauty is you.
An image of what God wants us to be.
Black is beautiful, black is excellent,
Black is evident, black is pain,
Black is suffering, black is everything.
Black is gold, black is magic,

Black is not a weakness,
Black is my superpower.
Being black means having to work twice as hard because of
the colour of my skin.
It means having to suffer in silence.
It means having to live with stereotypes
But knowing you're good enough
And that's why you exist.
It means having to embrace our colour,
That's why black is my superpower.

Munachi Unagha (14)
St Patrick's RC High School & Arts College, Eccles

Our Rubbish World

Temperatures fall and drop
Rubbish falls and drifts
Seas become emptier of fish
And animals starve and thirst
Flowers and trees are cut
Making the air dirtier
Making us sicker
All this because of our greedy nature.

Politicians embezzle, laugh and drink carefree
While the middle classes fight to keep afloat
Some sinking into despair, crying in an abandoned alley
When they lose their homes
And those they love
All this because of our greedy nature.

Or can we fix this
And right the wrongs we've caused?
We can fix this
We can plant trees
We can take care of creatures
Or we can watch as Earth becomes our rubbish world.

I hope we can change
For the good of the world

For the good of the people
And for the good of the creatures we live with
Or we can continue this rubbish existence.

Alex Sobczyk (11)
St Patrick's RC High School & Arts College, Eccles

Unbreakable

You may try to bring me down,
Scar me with your sharp words,
Wound me with your insults
But I will fly like birds,
I am unbreakable.
You may find it amusing,
To spread your twisted lies,
Pierce me with those hurtful and bitter threats.
Even though you may think you haunt me,
I will rise like butterflies.
Is this entertainment?
Fear, hurt and tearful eyes?
Feelings shattered like glass and dreams crushed?
I may be weakened by your careless cries,
But I will fight.
I am unbreakable.
Your comments hurt like an arrow to one's heart,
A dagger to the chest,
An everlasting burn.
But like a soldier, I will fight for what is right.
Does my presence offend your lonely heart?
Does my appearance upset you?
Submerged by the shame, the fear and the rumours.
Still, I stand, unbroken.
Because I am unbreakable.

Megan Cochrane (11)
St Patrick's RC High School & Arts College, Eccles

Without Education

The future depends on the next generation,
But how is that possible without education,
How can they teach the generation after that,
If jobs that require education, cannot deal with this
relentless combat?

In wartorn countries, children may not be safe,
They may feel imprisoned, unable to escape,
School is an escapism, from their harsh reality,
And brings them back to Earth
And some sort of normality.

Families in many cases have no choice,
In their situation, they have no voice.
It is their child's education or food on the table,
And if they choose education, it can make them unstable.

This situation is like dominoes,
We don't know how far it goes,
So why are we here waiting for this to happen?
We must go out, raise awareness and take action!

Katie Ratcliffe (13)
St Patrick's RC High School & Arts College, Eccles

Warfare Wishes

The war just started, how cold-hearted
Screams echo through the air, this isn't fair
Loud banging from afar, all night and day.
How I wish the sky wasn't grey.
Longing to play outside again, it's them to blame.
From my view it's a silly little thing.
What shame to bring.
Food running low, my energy is about to go.
I need to survive, so I can thrive.
The days go by, and I can fly
It's better here than living in fear.

Kyra Mason (12)
St Patrick's RC High School & Arts College, Eccles

Human

Two arms and legs
With which I stand,
Five fingers on each of my hands,
My head and heart ready to guide,
From morning till night you are by my side,
Oxygen in my lungs,
They breathe air,
Two colourful pools under my brows,
The translucent eyes forging a stare,
Two portable speakers held at my head,
A vacuum to trace scents
Gleaming on top of my beautiful hair,
Tied up or cut with whatever you wear.

Lourdez Francis (12)
St Patrick's RC High School & Arts College, Eccles

Our Natural Habitat

Our natural habitat,
It's becoming flat.
Eccles grows trees,
We fall on our knees.
We need to go,
As the cars blow.
Let's use sustainable energy,
For our children's standing.
Combine it into love,
Don't shove,
There's a better world next week,
For light may seek.
Forests are beautiful,
But our love is dull.
Say hello,
Let nature still grow.

Adrian Rojek (13)
St Patrick's RC High School & Arts College, Eccles

The Future Isn't Set In Stone

It isn't a done deal.
We need to change,
We need to try
And help the world,
Or in a couple of years we'll cry.
We need to change the world,
To make it great,
Before it's too late.
We need to work together as one,
As the future isn't set in stone.

Magdalena Goluchowska (14)
St Patrick's RC High School & Arts College, Eccles

Vanity

Vanity:
To admire one's own appearance
Not to shame or to shun
Not to blame or to run
Away from what's yours
So why do you call me vain?

Yes, I may pose
And fixate on my nose
But that should not propose
The idea that I chose
To be this way
Please do not assume I am vain.

To be vain is to stare
Out of love, out of care
But at myself, I glare
For I am the opposite of vain.

Each mirror reminds me
Not gently, but wisely
That I am in no place to feel nicely
About the body I am in
Oh, how I'd love to be vain.

But as a woman I am guided
As a woman I'm reminded
That I'll forever be provided
With reasons to be ashamed.

So please, call me Vain
As it seems to be my name
Watch it echo through the pain
Of carrying the weight of a woman -
A vessel of shame.

Connie Rushton (15)
The McAuley Catholic High School, Doncaster

God Complex

As the lines between God and mortal blur
And my words begin to slur,
Beneath my feet retreats the Earth I know
And I fall ever more to the abyss below.
My touch is lined with gold,
My love all but sold.
I hate this apathetic home,
A place so filthy, and morbidly prone,
To insatiable revenge that will clear,
A way to my throne that comes ever so near.
Under my hand, a kingdom will grow,
Because only I know,
My aim is to become a god,
Through this complex that will teach me only to tread,
Over the hearts that once never noticed my own.

Maja Lada (15)
The McAuley Catholic High School, Doncaster

War Waits For No One

As the coffin goes up,
The sound of explosions go down,
The people drinking from the glass cup,
See the picture-perfect, glass crown.

The violence that led these people away,
Suddenly froze in motion,
As the mourning began for a day,
The conflict was as still as an ocean.

But come 24 hours later,
The fire will still rage,
Because even the death of a queen couldn't cater,
The sign of peace on the page.

Lottie White (14)
The McAuley Catholic High School, Doncaster

It Is Fine

Say it's fine
Time goes by

Don't cry
Won't cry

Lie on my bed
Ceiling to my head

She's dead

It's not fine
It's not okay
All alone
Gone away

Lost, but never there
Never even brushed her hair
Never even touched her skin

Was her mum
But she's not her kin

Think it's gone
But then it stays
Years and months and months
And days
All but time was just a waste

Life and death
Death won the chase.

Georgie Pratt (16)
The McAuley Catholic High School, Doncaster

No To Bullying, Yes To Equality

We live in a world of discrimination,
Racism and sexism.
We live in a world where one difference makes you strange and bad.
Prejudiced...
Think your skin makes you scary
Your sex makes you silly
This is the world we live in today
But I hope tomorrow there will be equality,
Peace and kindness
Where people can feel safe
And not judged on the past
No racism, no sexism
And no discrimination, only equality.

Frankie Bergmanas (13)
The McAuley Catholic High School, Doncaster

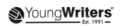 YoungWriters® Est. 1991

Young Writers Information

We hope you have enjoyed reading this book – and that you will continue to in the coming years.

If you're the parent or family member of an enthusiastic poet or story writer, do visit our website **www.youngwriters.co.uk/subscribe** and sign up to receive news, competitions, writing challenges and tips, activities and much, much more! There's lots to keep budding writers motivated!

If you would like to order further copies of this book, or any of our other titles, then please give us a call or order via your online account.

Young Writers
Remus House
Coltsfoot Drive
Peterborough
PE2 9BF
(01733) 890066
info@youngwriters.co.uk

Join in the conversation!
Tips, news, giveaways and much more!

 **YoungWritersUK**    **YoungWritersCW**   **youngwriterscw**